Be a Better Pharisee, or Quit Trying

Bill Kasper

You can purchase additional copies at www.createspace.com/5180338

For further studies on this and other topics, visit
www.overcominglaodicea.org

ISBN-13: 978-1-5086-1243-8
ISBN-10: 1-5086-1243-9

Contents

Introduction

The Wrong Reflection

You might be wondering: why write a book about the Pharisees? Well, this book is not really about the Pharisees we read about in the Bible. It's more about their way of thinking or what they represent. Many people think that the Pharisees are only a group of people who lived about 2,000 years ago during the time of Jesus. And yet, visit any church today, and you will see that the Pharisaical spirit is alive and well. They may not be a formally organized group with matching T-shirts, secret handshakes, or something similar, but it is possible to recognize their attitude in Christians anywhere.

You might not be particularly familiar with the Pharisees, but I imagine you would be able to recognize some of their characteristics. In fact, you may have even used the term "pharisaical" to describe a member of the church. But many of us, though we may not realize it, possess this same spirit in our own hearts. We can be pretty good at recognizing it in someone else, but have difficulty seeing it in ourselves. And not only in ourselves as individuals, but also within our own church or denomination. Especially within *our own* group. (It's sad how frequently we think *our* church/ group/ denomination is completely free of any human impurities. But *every* group filled with humans is susceptible to error.) In fact, we have been warned that there is a spirit of Pharisaism still present in our churches today. It is a self-satisfied attitude that believes that "there is no more light for the people of God."*

Yet, in my studies of this ancient group of religious leaders, to learn about their "spirit," I found something disconcerting: their reflection in my own life. When I took an honest look into my heart, I became aware that I was the Pharisee who wanted people to see my good works. I was that Pharisee who refused to be changed by the teachings of Christ. I was that Pharisee who was comfortable in the religion I was taught. I considered myself "good enough." It didn't help that people would tell me how good I was (how little did they really know me!). But I didn't enjoy seeing the pharisaical reflection in me; I wanted Jesus to be seen in me!

I also learned of Jesus' reaction to the Pharisees: their good wasn't good enough. As I read of how heaven's requirements were much greater than their "holiest" achievements, it became over-whelmingly apparent to me that my best wouldn't be good enough either. The more I studied, the more I understood the truth of what Jesus was teaching. I had to stop playing the Pharisees' game. I needed to quit trying to be a Pharisee.

I realize that you may have never given thought to the amount of "Pharisee" that may be reflected in you. Maybe you don't have any. If not, praise God! Keep following Jesus and only Jesus. But if, by some chance, there is even a little Pharisee in you, then my prayer is that this book will help you find out where their teachings have taken hold in your life and show you Jesus' solution—that, in the end, you will only find Jesus' reflection in you.

---

* Ellen G. White, *Counsels to Writers and Editors* (Nashville: Southern Publishing Association, 1946), 34. (See also quote on facing page.)

A spirit of pharisaism has been coming in upon the people who claim to believe the truth for these last days. They are self-satisfied. They have said, "We have the truth. There is no more light for the people of God." But we are not safe when we take a position that we will not accept anything else than that upon which we have settled as truth. We should take the Bible, and investigate it closely for ourselves. . . .

We have many lessons to learn, and many, many to unlearn. God and heaven alone are infallible. Those who think that they will never have to give up a cherished view, never have occasion to change an opinion, will be disappointed. As long as we hold to our own ideas and opinions with determined persistency, we cannot have the unity for which Christ prayed.

– ELLEN WHITE,
Counsels to Writers and Editors, p. 34, 37.

Chapter One

"For I tell you that unless your righteousness
surpasses that of the Pharisees and the teachers of the law,
you will certainly not enter the kingdom of heaven."
– MATTHEW 5:20

Artificial Preservatives

What is the first thought that comes to your mind when the word "Pharisee" is mentioned? Is it a positive or a negative thought? Maybe I should ask it another way: would you want to be labeled a Pharisee? Your answer would reveal your feelings toward the title. Most people today would rather not be called a Pharisee.

Look up the adjective "Pharisaical" in any dictionary and you will find it typically defined by words like "hypocritical" and "self-righteous." In our day, the term is regularly viewed in a negative light. Interestingly, this is quite different from what you would find in the *Concise Dictionary of Judaism*. It says that they "represented the finest tradition of their people and of human morals."* It is evident that much has happened to change our perception of this group.

The Pharisees had noble beginnings.† Their roots seem to go back to their time in Babylonian and Persian captivity. As the people of Israel began to pick up the pagan practices and beliefs of their captors, a group of loyal Israelites dedicated themselves to upholding their traditions and beliefs. Then, around 168 BC, out of the wars during the time of Antiochus Epiphanes and Judas Maccabaeus, we find the first mention of a party named Pharisees, which meant "separated ones."

Although they faced some difficulties, by the time Jesus was born they were established as a strong political party and religious authority. They were considered national heroes. They were known to be careful students of scripture. They were strict, disciplined, and traditional. They sat in the seat of Moses and were viewed as the final authority on Scripture, which resulted from their deep love for the law of God and their desire to uphold it. Such a group of spiritual leaders would be honored and admired by Christians even today!

Of course, out of their deep love for God's law came a great desire to protect it. Therefore, they created doctrinal "fences," through additional rules and regulations, to prevent Israel from getting too close to breaking God's law and potentially angering Him. The people of Israel had a well-documented history of falling away from God. Because of this, the Pharisees felt that guidance was required to keep it from ever happening again. As a result, hundreds of additional laws were written. If the people would follow these laws, they would be guaranteed a safe distance away from transgressing God's law. The Pharisees believed that they could preserve their nation from God's anger—that they could save their people from future errors and destruction.

At first, these laws were simply meant for guidance, but soon it became evident that they were no longer optional and, in some cases, were considered even more important than God's law. Since the people could not be trusted to apply Scripture's principles on their own, the leaders believed they needed to apply the principles for them. Inevitably, the Pharisees became seen as *the* example of righteousness for Israel: follow their rules and, with any luck, you might achieve their level of holiness and receive God's reward.

Enter Jesus. He knew the ways of the Pharisees. He knew their love for the law and their contempt for anyone who was against it. So, He reassured the people, especially the Pharisees, that He was not there to be against the law, but to fully keep it.

> Do not think that I have come to abolish the Law or the Prophets; I have come not to abolish them but to fulfill them. I tell you the truth, until heaven and earth disappear, not the smallest letter, not the least stroke of a pen, will by any means disappear from the Law until everything is accomplished. Anyone who breaks one of the least of these commandments and teaches others to do the same will be called least in the kingdom of heaven, but whoever practices and teaches these commands will be called great in the kingdom of heaven. (Matthew 5:17–19)

It even sounded like He was commending the Pharisees for their efforts! They must have delighted in that last statement that "whoever practices and teaches these commands will be called great in the kingdom of heaven." He called them great! They were the teachers of the law, were they not? They were the example of strict obedience to the law. To those listening that day, it would seem that Jesus just gave His official support to the Pharisees. How wonderful!

But Jesus wasn't finished: "For I tell you that unless your righteousness surpasses that of the Pharisees and the teachers of the law, you will certainly not enter the kingdom of heaven" (verse 20).

Now you may not find this statement shocking, but it should be—it would have been for everyone in that group. We would naturally assume the Pharisees didn't care for it, but it would have been hard for even a regular Jew to process as well. The Pharisees were their example for righteousness. I'm sure you can think of people whom you admire as being good Christians. You may even secretly wish that you could be as spiritually strong as them. You wouldn't hesitate to label them godly. This is how most people in

Israel thought of the Pharisees. And now Jesus was saying that their righteousness must be greater than that of their illustrious human examples? Not simply equal to, but *surpassing* it! If the leadership who strictly kept the law weren't righteous enough, then *who could be?*

This was the group that had introduced, and rigorously kept, a rigid standard. They had embraced, as Paul called it, a legalistic righteousness (Philippians 3:6); it was a righteousness earned through keeping the law—a righteousness created by them. But how well did their Pharisaical righteousness fare from God's point of view? In Matthew 23:28, Jesus told them that "on the outside you appear to people as righteous but on the inside you are full of hypocrisy and wickedness." Ouch.

If what the Pharisees were living wasn't righteousness, what *is* righteousness? To many today, it is an indefinable spiritual state we must attain to be saved. Some may describe it as perfectly keeping God's law. Yet, the Bible is very clear that this isn't the case. In Romans 3:20 Paul says that, "no one will be declared righteous in his [God's] sight by observing the law, rather through the law we become conscious of sin."

But then, if righteousness isn't keeping the law, what is? The original words used in these texts, both Greek and Hebrew, have two basic meanings: righteousness and justice—being in the right and being just. This definition places more emphasis on choices. This should be easy enough for us, shouldn't it? We can make right choices, can't we?

Unfortunately, we cannot. We are told in Isaiah 64:6 that our "righteousness is but filthy rags [bloodied garments]." Psalm 14:3 declares that "there is no one who does good, not even one." And Ecclesiastes 7:20 says, "There is not a righteous man on earth who does what is right and never sins." Not a good picture it's painting of us, is it? Solomon helps to shed some light on our predicament. He says, "There is a way that seems right to a man, but in the end it leads to death" (Proverbs 14:12). Jesus also said that "what is highly valued by man is detestable in God's sight" (Luke

16:15). In other words, by default, we do not make the right choices. According to this, we cannot trust our choices when it comes to spiritual or eternal issues.

This brings us back to our initial problem: if we can't be better than the Pharisees, what can we do? Much of our time is wasted trying to compete spiritually with each other because many have taken Jesus' comment as a challenge to surpass the Pharisees at their own game. Yet, the Bible is clear that there is a definite limit to human righteousness (which the Pharisees strived to obtain and offered as an example to the people), and that limit is always below God's standard. Instead, we need to pay closer attention to what Jesus is saying. His suggestion: quit trying. The truth is, in order to surpass them in righteousness, we can't play their games.

God says, "Come now, let us reason together, though your sins are like scarlet [bloodied garments], they shall be as white as snow [white garments]; though they are red as crimson, they shall be like wool" (Isaiah 1:18). He wants to *give us* righteousness! He wants us to give up our own "righteousness" and accept that which He offers. This is what Jesus was talking about; this is the reason He counsels each one of us to "seek first the Kingdom of God, and His righteousness" (Matthew 6:33). In order to do this though, we must stop trying to be like the Pharisees and accept a righteousness that is much greater than theirs.

Notice how His righteousness is described: Psalm 119:142 says, "Your righteousness is everlasting and your law is true." And Psalm 145:17 says, "The Lord is righteous in ALL his ways, and loving toward all he has made." How many of us can say that we are right all the time in all of our ways? Yet, the Bible says that God is always righteous—always right, always just. Why? This is what Jeremiah 11:20 says: "But, O LORD Almighty, you who judge righteously and test the heart and mind."

Here is the difference: He can always choose right, or judge right, because He knows *why*. He knows our deepest thoughts and secrets—including our motives. Our choices and judgment will always be wrong because all we can ever see is exterior "works."

We often pick on those obvious sins we can see, yet neglect the larger sins that will destroy us. We have it all mixed up. We label visible "perfections" as godly, and surface "imperfections" as sin. It wouldn't surprise me if some today might actually believe that Satan was kicked out of heaven for smoking near the throne! Yet, the Bible is clear: the obvious, outward "sins" we see are not as important as what God sees in the heart.

The good news is that God wants to give us something better: His righteousness. He wants to give us right choices, not simply right actions. He wants to establish *His* will in our lives.

This is what Paul chose. According to him, by all "church" standards he had been perfect; he was a true Hebrew, a great Pharisee, and flawless in legalistic righteousness (see Philippians 3:3–11). That is some bragging! However, he considered all of that worthless in the light of knowing Christ. What he used to be was no longer what he wanted to be. He wanted to gain Christ, and be found in *His* righteousness. But how can Christ just give us His righteousness? Paul explains in Romans 5:18, 19:

> Consequently, just as the result of one trespass was condemnation for all men, so also the result of one act of righteousness was justification that brings life for all men. For just as through the disobedience of the one man the many were made sinners, so also through the obedience of the one man the many will be made righteous.

Amazingly, Jesus' sinless obedience—His right choices and righteous living—can be credited to us. And, believe it or not, it is also a free gift! "For it is by grace you have been saved, through faith—and this not from yourself, it is the *gift of God*" (Ephesians 2:8, emphasis mine).

You may be wondering, if Jesus' obedience is credited to me, then does it matter what I do? Habakkuk 2:4 says, "The righteous will live by faith." Hosea 14:9 says it this way: "The ways of the Lord are right; the righteous walk in them." Yes it does matter!

You see, now, instead of living life by your own choices (by law), you will live by God's choices (by faith). You are not merely following rules anymore; you are following your God wherever *He* leads. This is a change from living according to your will to living according to His will. Paul describes such a life this way: "I have been crucified with Christ and I no longer live, but *Christ lives in me*. The life I live in the body, I live by faith in the Son of God, who loved me and gave Himself for me" (Galatians 2:20, emphasis mine). This is what it means to "trust in the Lord with all your heart and lean not on your own understanding" (Proverbs 3:5). Accepting Christ's righteousness is letting Him make decisions for your life. He is not copilot, but Pilot; not casual observer, but sole decision maker. It is a righteousness that comes from complete dependence on God and from passionately following Him. This is the same righteousness Jesus promises to provide us. It is not life support—not an artificial preservative—but a life more abundant!

No doubt, there will be some of you who are still skeptical. Some of you who believe you know best for your life; you are confident in your ability to make the right decisions. For those who have this confidence, I offer this parable from Jesus:

He told of two men going to the temple to pray, a Pharisee and a tax collector. The Pharisee stood proud and prayed about his accomplishments. It was more of a bragging session before God—a look-what-I've-done monologue. His works had set him apart and he was proud of them. The tax collector, however, tried to avoid detection. He couldn't even look up. He was there for one reason only: he was a sinner and he knew it. So, he pled for mercy from God. Jesus concluded by saying, "I tell you that this man, rather than the other, went home justified before God. For everyone who exalts himself will be humbled, and he who humbles himself will be exalted" (Luke 18:14).

Do not miss the point: the moment you become confident in your own righteousness, you no longer think you need a savior. If it was possible to work your way to heaven, Jesus died for nothing (Galatians 2:21)! Friend, don't be deceived. The Bible says, "You who are trying to be justified by law have been alienated from Christ; you have fallen away from grace" (Galatians 5:4).

Maybe you've been encouraged to believe that your good works are enough. While you may appear holy to others on the outside, to God you're spiritually dead on the inside. This is the result of trying to be a Pharisee, and it is not enough. So quit trying. And, instead, accept the hope that God offers:

> But, when the kindness and love of God our Savior appeared, he saved us, not because of righteous things we had done, but because of his mercy. He saved us through the washing of rebirth and renewal by the Holy Spirit, whom he poured out on us generously through Jesus Christ our Savior, so that, having been justified by his grace, we might become heirs having the hope of eternal life. (Titus 3:4-7)

If you become consumed by the idea that you have to achieve personal perfection in obedience to God's law, you will find yourself constantly doubting your salvation. But salvation is not about you—what you have or have not done—but about God and His mercy and grace. It is not about your righteousness, but His. So, accept His gift; let Him lead you in the paths of *His* righteousness. Follow Him. Trust Him! Because He offers true life—life more abundant—life eternal!

---

* Dagobert D. Runes, ed., *Concise Dictionary of Judaism* (New York: Philosophical Library, 1959), 184.

† William L. Coleman, *The Pharisees' Guide to Total Holiness* (Minneapolis: Bethany House Publishers, 1977), 17–24.

Chapter Two

"So whether you eat or drink or whatever you do,
do it all for the glory of God."
— 1 CORINTHIANS 10:31

The Greatest Show on Earth

It may have only been a few minutes, but to me it seemed like hours. All my attempts at communication had gone unnoticed. I had been practicing for quite a while and was now prepared to reveal my newly perfected talent. But I had a problem: no one was watching! Was I doing this for nothing? Was I doing all of this work, only to have no one see it?

I'm sure I am not the only person to have gone through such agony. Perhaps you have gone through the anguish of reaching a new level of personal achievement, only to have no one notice. Like making a hole-in-one with no one around to witness it or getting a fancy new haircut that no one *ahem* mentions. Like mastering a difficult musical piece, when no one shows up for the concert; or finally overcoming your most obvious bad habit, but no one in the church notices.

How could they not notice? How *dare* they not notice! All of my waving, all of my yelling—my efforts to grab their attention had gone on so long, my voice was actually beginning to fail. Soon, I would not even be able to speak. Did they not know how extremely important this was? I was about to do something great! I knew they would be proud; I was sure they'd be happy. So, there I sat, on top of the slide at my great aunt's pool, waiting for mom and dad to notice.

Children thrive in their parents' happiness. To see the smile on the face of their parent only pushes them to greater things. So when a child says, "Did you *see* what I've just done?" we respond, "how cute!" (Of course, parents can get *really* excited about the most unusual things their child does "by themselves"—going potty, for example.) But for some reason, this changes as we get older. Have an adult come up to you and also say, "Did you see what *I've* just done?" and we'll respond, "what a show-off!" No one (that I know of) looks forward to listening to others list off their many "great" accomplishments. As they brag, their speech can end up sounding like one of the adults from the Charlie Brown cartoons. You may find yourself half smiling while unconsciously nodding your head, which they think is in agreement to their greatness, but you are actually hoping a friend will come to rescue you. It's horrible, isn't it? Now, as hard as it may be, try to imagine what this kind of bragging might sound like . . . if it happened at your church!

Unfortunately, moments of bragging do occur in the church. And it occurred in the church in Jesus' day. There were some who wanted everyone to see their great spiritual accomplishments. Jesus talks about them in Matthew 23:

> Everything they do is done for men to see: They make their phylacteries [*a small leather case worn on the arm and forehead, especially when praying*] wide and the tassels on their garments long; they love the place of honor at banquets and the most important seats in the synagogues;

they love to be greeted in the marketplaces and to have men call them "Rabbi." (Verses 5–7)

Speaking of the Pharisees, He said that they do everything so that men will notice. All of the things they held dear—position, recognition, titles—are what men notice. These are things the Pharisees viewed and taught as evidence of spiritual success. Not surprisingly, those ideals are *still* valued and emphasized today among Christians.

But Jesus said that the Pharisees only *looked* holier because they drew attention to their actions or greatly exaggerated their standards. When they gave their offering, or fasted, they would put on a big show so people would notice. When they prayed, they'd use long prayers with big words to impress (glad *that* doesn't happen in our churches today!). Ultimately, since they were the models of holiness, if they appeared one step higher than the people, they had authority over the people. If they said that something made a person more holy, the people believed it or risked being cut from membership. John 12:42, 43 says that "many even among the leaders believed in [Jesus]. But because of the Pharisees they would not confess their faith for fear they would be put out of the synagogue; for they loved [*agapaō*] praise from men more than praise from God."

The Greek verb *agapaō* translated "love" contains the idea of placing someone or something first in one's affections. It is also commonly defined as unconditional love. This means that the Pharisees placed praise from men first in their affection—they loved it unconditionally. They didn't care who it was coming from or even if it was real praise. False praise was better than no praise.

Sadly, long after the oppression of those Pharisees, people still lived in fear of losing the leaders' praise. They did whatever they could to keep, or exceed, the church's approval. One man, Simeon the Stylite, tried to avoid being defiled by the evils of the world by separating himself and living on top of a 15 meter tall pillar for 39 years until his death in 459 (and he still holds the record in the 2010

Guinness World Book of Records for longest pole sit!"). Before he learned about justification by faith, Martin Luther, in order to stay pure by keeping his fleshly desires in control, beat himself morning and evening. In the late 1800s, Advent "Spiritualizers" were told that they must be like little children to be in the kingdom of heaven, so they proceeded to crawl everywhere and stopped using forks and knives when they ate. In Israel today, it is considered unholy to turn your back on a holy place, like the Western wall in Jerusalem. Thus a "holy" person would back away out of respect and then turn and go. However, a *holier* individual would back even *further* before turning—even a half a mile away. All of this, just to stay approved by the church and appear holy in the eyes of man.

The Pharisees' attitude continues to have an influence in our own churches. We often set up our own holiness "standard," and as a result, we struggle to meet the expectations of the church and each other, even to the point of competition. But Jesus confronts this pharisaic example when He says, "You are the ones who *justify yourselves in the eyes of men*, but God knows your hearts. What is highly valued among men is detestable in God's sight" (Luke 16:15, emphasis mine). All of their actions were to justify themselves—to make themselves righteous—in man's opinion. But Jesus says that these standards, which we think justify us before God, are actually detestable (lit. an abomination) to God!

Consider this question God asked Israel: "When you fasted and mourned in the fifth and seventh months for the past seventy years, was it really for me that you fasted? And when you were eating and drinking, were you not just feasting for yourselves?" (Zechariah 7:5, 6). In other words, for *whom* are you doing all of this? All of your church attendance, all of your offerings, all of your songs, all of your prayers and ministries and socials and seminars—are they really for God? Or are they done for *you*?

Have you ever asked yourself this question? Are you doing these things to obtain God's approval or to gain another person's approval? Could it be so that *others* might notice and you could *appear* a bit holier than you really are?

You might be wondering if it really matters for whom you do it as long as you do it. Paul thought so. This is what he says: "Am I now trying to win the approval of man, or of God? Or, am I trying to please men? If I were still trying to please men, I would not be a servant of Christ" (Galatians 1:10). Does it really matter? Yes, of course it matters! You cannot strive to please man and still be a servant of Christ. This means that you are not a Christian if you care more about what man thinks of you than what God thinks of you. Alarming isn't it?

Yet, it makes sense doesn't it? If I am truly following Christ, then I will want to please *Him*. This is the reason Peter writes that everything we do should be done for God, so that "in all things God may be praised through Jesus Christ" (1 Peter 4:11). And Paul says, "So whether you eat or drink or whatever you do, do it all for the glory of God" (1 Corinthians 10:31). This means that we are not doing things so *we* will get recognition and praise, but so *God* will get recognition and praise. It is about God, not us.

Jesus taught this concept often. He instructed those following Him to watch the motives of their actions (see Matthew 6:1-8). Whether acts of righteousness or prayer, Jesus warned that if we do these things just so we can be seen by men, we have no reward with God. In fact, if we are only seeking the praise of man, when we receive that praise it will be all we receive—nothing more. Of course, when you think of it in the scope of eternity, it is nothing. Just empty praise. Even if every person in your church is pleased about what you are doing, what value does it have if God is not pleased? Instead, Jesus tells us not to be seen, but to be hidden. We are not to "toot our own horn." We are not to promote our name (or our church's). Because, when you are doing things for God, then it doesn't matter if man sees *you*. If God is to be praised, it isn't important that you receive credit. As Paul says, you serve "as if you were serving the Lord, not men" (Ephesians 6:7).

You may wonder, what about our standards? The church has standards that we're bound to, aren't we? This is frequently a sticky subject. On one hand, when the church teaches a solid biblical principle, it benefits us if we listen and follow. On the other hand, not everything taught in churches today has biblical support. Some standards have come from our own "wisdom." Paul calls these teachings "hollow and deceptive philosophy, which depends on human tradition and the basic principles of this world rather than on Christ" (Colossians 2:8). They will come and go since they are based on fickle human wisdom. And while they may seem good and even "holy" on the surface—with regulated worship and false humility—they lack value in the eyes of God (Colossians 2:20–23). How could even our best rules bring us closer to God? Remember: Jesus said that what we value, God detests.

Whether we like to hear this or not, Paul says that although many of *our* standards, which are meant to purify us (on the outside), may seem right, they do not get rid of the source of the problem (on the inside). You may cut the leaves off the tree, but unless you destroy the root, the leaves will grow back. This isn't to say that all church teachings are wrong and should be thrown out, but principles *based on our wisdom* will always fail to bring true spiritual change, so essentially, we do them in vain. Notice Paul's recommendation: "Since, then, you have been raised with Christ, set your hearts on things above, where Christ is seated at the right hand of God. Set your minds on things above, not on earthly things. For you died, and your life is now hidden with Christ in God" (Colossians 3:1–3).

Don't look to man for the standard of holiness, look above—to Christ. Our Savior calls us to a higher standard than man does: He calls us to follow *Him*. To live, not just *for* Christ, but *hidden in* Christ. Living in a way in which we aren't seen, but He is.

This is the ultimate game of Hide-and-Seek. The rules are simple: you hide while someone "seeks" you. In this classic game, you win by not being found. The better you hide, the longer you last and more likely you are to win. The best hiders are able to find an unsuspecting place in which no one can find them. I remember hiding once in our dryer. It was difficult getting into it—I barely fit—but I knew that no one would look there. Sure enough, after several minutes the one seeking gave up. I wasn't found because all they saw was the dryer, not me. Unfortunately, I had been hiding in there so long my legs fell asleep and I couldn't get the door back open. I had to get their attention to rescue me from my hiding place. I was so well hidden I couldn't even escape!

So, how does a life look that is hidden in Christ? *You* would be entirely hidden from sight—your selfishness, desires, and pride—and the only thing showing would be Christ. In everything you do, people would see the character of Jesus. You would be "clothed" in His compassion, kindness, humility, gentleness, and patience. You would be forgiving and loving towards each other. People would only see the character of Jesus, not you. Everything you do would be in the name of Jesus (Colossians 3:12-17). Not your name, not the church's name, but Jesus' name. He gets the glory. He gets the praise.

Followers of Christ *should* be doing praiseworthy things, but who ultimately gets the praise? Examine your "good things." For whom are *you* doing all these Christian acts? Are you standing in the synagogue for all to see, or are you hidden in Christ?

Pharisees try to please men and gain their approval. So they will attempt to put on the greatest show Christianity has ever seen—hoping that *they* will be seen. Of course, each time the show will have to become more grand. To make matters worse, it will also get harder and harder to put on a good show, because someone will eventually show you up.

So quit trying; quit trying to gain man's praise and instead seek only God's. Imagine what could happen in your life, in your work, and even in your church, if you lived for God's praise rather than man's praise? Why should we care what man thinks? Hide yourself in Jesus! *To Him be the glory and the power for ever and ever, Amen!*

---

* *Guinness World Records 2010*, (New York: Bantam Books, 2009), xxiv. It is their longest unbroken record, having been unbroken for 1,500 years.

Chapter Three

"Do not judge, and you will not be judged. Do not condemn,
and you will not be condemned. Forgive, and you will be
forgiven. Give, and it will be given to you. A good measure,
pressed down, shaken together and running over,
will be poured into your lap. For with the measure you use, it
will be measured to you."

– LUKE 6:37, 38

Romancing the Stones

I have had to be a part of what I feel is the worst thing a pastor ever has to do: church discipline. Some pastors may enjoy it, but I do not. The following story illustrates why: A man in my church had been accused of a fairly serious criminal charge, and although he claimed he was innocent, he had no witnesses and no alibi. Soon, his situation was brought before the church board with a demand that something should be done. Some wanted him to be removed from membership right then and there. Eventually, however, we came to the decision that since he would be going to court, we would let the court decide his innocence and then act accordingly. If he was found guilty, we would proceed with church discipline. If he was found innocent, he would be fully reinstated. In the meantime, we would have him temporarily step down from any leadership positions he had in the church.

After some time (in our "speedy" justice system), his day to appear in court came. It didn't last long though. Moments after the trial began, all charges were dropped. His accuser *admitted* to making up the whole thing. In other words, he was truly innocent and free to go! According to the courts, and his accuser, no crime had been committed. The church board reconvened at the church and I announced the court's decision: he was innocent and the charges had been dropped. Praise the Lord!

A few of the board members reacted by saying, "Yes, but . . ." But? I was shocked that there was still a debate about whether to restore his position in the church. The accuser even admitted the accusation was a lie. This was the explanation I was given: "But he was accused. He has been in court. What affect will that have on our reputation as a church? If someone were to see him leading up front, imagine the damage it could do to us!" Because of this outspoken few, the board, unfortunately, was not willing to accept his innocence and pushed to remove him permanently from all of his leadership positions in church.

Why are we so hasty to judge? Especially judging down. It seems that many Christians are overly eager to find something wrong in another person. This apple does not fall far from the tree that is the Pharisees. Consider the following story recorded in the Gospel of John (see John 8:3–11).

Jesus had come to the temple one day and, as usual, people came to see Him. Not one to pass up an opportunity, He began to teach them. It is in this scene that the story takes place: at church with a large group of people. Then *they* showed up. The Bible says that the Pharisees arrived with a woman and placed her in the middle of the group—the very place where Jesus was standing. Throwing her to the ground, they stated that the woman before them was a sinner and had been caught in adultery. In fact, the Bible says she was *seized* in the very act of adultery. This was not hearsay—not the result of gossip-gone-wild—she was caught *while* committing the crime. It was an obvious sin, the easiest kind in which to catch people.

Immediately, red flags pop up in their story. How *did* they catch her? How could they know she would be where she was, at that moment, doing what she was doing? It was not as if, by some good fortune, they were walking by and said, "Hey, I hear adultery happening!" Had they been watching, waiting for her to sin so they could catch her? It sounds suspicious. It sounds like a set-up. Spiritual leaders setting up someone to sin—how sick is that? But they didn't leave any time for anyone to ponder this and went straight to the question. "In the Law Moses commanded us to stone such women. Now what do you say?" (John 8:5).

Well wasn't that thoughtful? Turns out, they were simply being good Israelites. They were only concerned about the law, because "in the Law Moses *commanded*." But what would Jesus have them do? Well, it is true that Leviticus 20:10 and Deuteronomy 22:22 both say, "If a man is found sleeping with another man's wife, both the man who slept with her and the woman must die." Couldn't argue with that, could you? The law said she had to die. She must be stoned. (Some people sure love those stones, don't they?)

But wait, something in the scenario was wrong again: where was the guy? If this were only about upholding the law, then why would they not have brought the man to justice? Surely, if this was about the integrity of the law, then *everyone* guilty should be brought to be stoned, right? (Maybe he *was* there, hidden in the crowd, watching this all take place.) Obviously, this was not about the law. This was not even about the woman. Their true motive is revealed in verse six: "They were using this question as a trap, in order to have a basis for accusing him."

This episode was entirely about trapping Jesus. They wanted evidence that could accuse Him. They were looking for something to knock Jesus off His pedestal. But of course! He *was* getting too "holy." Before Jesus came on the scene, *they* had influence—*they* were respected. But now, *His* influence and respect was growing greater than theirs. This had to stop! They were even ready to kill this woman, just to keep their influence. They were ready to stone her to bring Jesus down. No, it was not about the law, or the woman—it was about them. So they designed a trap. There was no way He could win. He could not choose to save this woman and still uphold the law. They had Him either way! [*Cue evil laugh.*]

But Jesus didn't answer their question. Instead, He bent down and started writing on the ground with His finger. He seemingly ignored the question and literally wrote on the ground. I'm sure His reaction infuriated the Pharisees. There's nothing worse than being ignored—especially during a well-planned trap! So, they bugged Him further, demanding an answer. This was the answer they got: "If any one of you is without sin, let him be first to throw a stone at her" (John 8:7).

They weren't expecting that. Who hasn't sinned? In spite of how they appeared to live, they experienced the truth Paul would later write about in Romans 3:23: "All have sinned and fallen short of the glory of God." The Pharisees no doubt felt that Jesus was not being fair. Only those who have never sinned can condemn a sinner? How could they uphold *their* laws when Jesus said this? Of course, it is as Paul says in Romans 2:1, "You, therefore, have no excuse, you who pass judgment on someone else, for at whatever point you judge the other, you are condemning yourself, because you who pass judgment do the same things."

As quickly as He had stood up, Jesus returned to His knees and continued writing on the ground. Maybe He was writing their sins—specific enough that each would recognize that Jesus knew their hearts. Maybe He was writing out scriptures like Jeremiah 2:35, "You say I am innocent; he is not angry with me. But I will pass judgment on you because you say, 'I have not sinned.'" Or Ezekiel 35:11, "I will treat you in accordance with the anger and jealousy you showed in your hatred of them and I will make myself known among them when I judge you." Perhaps He wrote from the very law they loved written in Deuteronomy 19:18, 19, which says that if someone wrongly accuses someone else, they are to receive the punishment meant for the one wrongly accused.

It doesn't really matter what He was writing. Whatever He was writing was being written in the dirt, and that which is written in dirt can be erased. Whatever it was, though, His writing caught their attention. Beginning with the older, wiser ones, their hearts became convicted and they slowly left—one by one—until only Jesus stood there with the woman (John 8:9).

Imagine what this woman must have been feeling this whole time. Curled up on the ground, cringing in expectation of the first stone, she was at their mercy. And it sounded like Jesus just gave the Pharisees permission to stone her! Her fate was sealed. She knew, as did all the others in the crowd, that the Pharisees were as close to perfection as humanly possible.

The first stone would hit soon. It would all be over shortly.

She didn't know they were *leaving*.

Having responded to the question of the Pharisees, He turned His attention to the woman: "Woman, where are they? Has no one condemned you?" (John 8:10). What? She was caught in the act! Of course she was condemned. The Pharisees condemned her. The law condemned her. Her very actions condemned her! Yet Jesus asked, "Has *no one* condemned you?"

She slowly looked up through the blurriness of tears, expecting judgmental stares. "No one, sir."

"*Then neither do I condemn you*" (John 8:11).

Wow. Jesus was full of surprises! He was the only one with the true right to throw a stone yet He doesn't. Why not? Because that was not why He was here. Jesus had explained His purpose on earth earlier: "For God so loved the world that he gave his only son that whoever believes in him will not perish but have eternal life. For God did not send his son into the world to condemn the world, but to save the world through him" (John 3:16, 17).

"*Then neither do I condemn you.*" Imagine the joy she must have felt hearing those words! The leadership condemned her, but Jesus didn't. She deserved death; He gave her mercy. Even so, mercy is not without redirection—as Jesus said, "go now and leave your life of sin" (John 8:11). He offered her something she didn't deserve (according to the law): a second chance. Although He did not condemn her, He did not want to leave her in her sins either.

Jesus came to save us and this means He must often redirect us, correct us, and change us.

The Bible says we are wise to listen to and accept correction from God and each other (see Ecclesiastes 7:5; Proverbs 12:1; Matthew 18:15). So yes, we should help each other out. We should hold each other accountable and give correction. But this is not judging. There is a difference: one encourages growth now; the other is a verdict for eternity.

However, doesn't the Bible say in 1 Corinthians 6:2, 3 that the saints will one day judge angels and the world? Absolutely! Just remember, it says that we *will* judge. Also, 1 Corinthians 4:5 warns us not to judge too soon: "Therefore judge nothing before the appointed time; wait till the Lord comes. He will bring to light what is hidden in darkness and will expose the motives of men's hearts." True and just judgment requires having all the information. One day, you will be given all of the information necessary to make the right judgment. Paul says to wait until then.

Furthermore, Jesus' correction is not judgment—He says He didn't come to condemn. He is not the one accusing us (John 5:45). Our accuser is revealed in Revelation:

> The great dragon was hurled down—that ancient serpent called the devil, or Satan, who leads the world astray. He was hurled to the earth, and his angels with him. Then I heard a loud voice in heaven say: "Now have come salvation and the power and the kingdom of our God, and the authority of his Christ. For the accuser of our brothers, who accuses them before our God day and night, has been hurled down." (Revelation 12:9, 10)

Satan actually means "adversary, accuser." Ever since his fall, he has mastered the art of accusing. He accuses both God and man. Therefore, when we behave as an accuser we are, in reality, following Satan's example not Christ's. To be Christlike requires us to show mercy.

It is said of God in Micah 7:18, "Who is a God like you, who pardons sin and forgives the transgression of the remnant of his inheritance? You do not stay angry forever but delight to show mercy." What's more, according to Hosea 6:6, God desires "mercy, not sacrifice." And Jesus explained in Matthew 12:7 that if we truly understood these words in Hosea, we "would not have condemned the innocent."

I know there are still some who love those stones. The way the stones feel in the hand; the thrill of anticipation at being able to throw it at some deserving miscreant. Sometimes we can be all too eager to find a fault to condemn in those around us. Yet, there is not a single story in the Bible of Jesus throwing a stone. Sure, He has said tough things to people (especially the Pharisees), but He was hardest on those who claimed to be holy, not those who admitted to being sinners. No, Jesus' ministry was full of mercy and grace towards the worst of sinners.

You see, this is what it comes down to: a Pharisee is quick to accusations and judgment, while Christ is quick to mercy and forgiveness. And you will be like one or the other. It's your choice. But before you make your choice, think about what Jesus says:

> Do not judge, and you will not be judged. Do not condemn, and you will not be condemned. Forgive, and you will be forgiven. Give, and it will be given to you. A good measure, pressed down, shaken together and running over, will be poured into your lap. For with the measure you use, it will be measured to you. (Luke 6:37, 38)

He says that you will be judged *by God* according to how you judge others. Furthermore, you will be forgiven *by God* according to your willingness to forgive others. This may seem severe, even unbelievable, but can we expect anything else? If we are unwilling to show mercy to others, why would we expect anyone to show us mercy? Jesus leaves no room for doubt on this matter, "if you do not forgive others their sins, your Father will not forgive your sins" (Matthew 6:15). These passages are basically saying that when our case comes before God in heaven we will be shown the same amount of mercy that we have shown to others. In other words, our behavior towards each other will be the measuring stick for the amount of grace, mercy and forgiveness we will receive from God.

For some reason, we have been taught that we have more power when we judge, but the Bible teaches differently. James 2:13 says, "judgment without mercy will be shown to anyone who has not been merciful. Mercy triumphs over [lit. is more powerful than] judgment" (notes mine). Take a moment to let this sink in: mercy *is more powerful than* judgment. You see, anyone can point out another person's obvious mistakes, but there is no power in that. Showing someone mercy? Now *that's* power.

So, whom do you resemble: the accuser of the brethren or the God of Mercy? God forbid that we might ever again act as the Pharisee and reflect the Accuser! May we be like Christ!

Chapter Four

"This is what the LORD says, 'Let not the wise man boast of his wisdom or the strong man boast of his strength or the rich man boast of his riches, but let him who boasts boast about this: that he understands and knows me, that I am the LORD, who exercises kindness, justice and righteousness on earth, for in these I delight,' declares the LORD."

– JEREMIAH 9:23, 24

Are You Smarter Than a Pharisee?

W*elcome back!*

Before we begin today, let's take a moment to get to know our contestants.

Our first contestant is the returning champion, Gamaliel. A leader among leaders, Gamaliel is one of the most respected individuals to ever participate. He is well established in the scholarly world as one of the top Pharisees of this century. A major contributor to the highly esteemed Pharisaical laws and doctrine, he is definitely the strongest contestant coming into today's competition.

Next, we have Jacob ben-Jonah. Born in the beautiful north side of Jerusalem to well-respected parents, Jacob is the top graduate in his class, achieving some of the highest test scores ever recorded. An accomplished competitor, there is little question of his bright future as a Teacher of the Law, since he has already received a number of incredible offers from several major synagogues.

Finally, we have Jesus ben-Joseph. Jesus only recently popped up on the radar screen, but has quickly grown in popularity. Little is known of him, other than that he seems to have been home-schooled in the ghettos of Nazareth. In spite of the mystery that has enveloped him, he has shown himself to be full of surprises. Still, with no formal education or position to speak of, he is undoubtedly the underdog in today's competition.

Now that we have met our contestants, let's get ready to play, "Are you smarter than a Pharisee?"

Sounds silly, doesn't it? Yet, this sort of mindset is exactly what Jesus experienced regularly, along with many other people in those days. The Pharisees and teachers of the law took pride in the fact that they had a more complete comprehension of biblical things. Few dared to, or even could, confront their scriptural knowledge. It is not surprising that this mindset existed. Starting from that one tree in the Garden of Eden, mankind has always been chasing after greater "knowledge." It can also be seen these days in our games, in our work, in our schools and, unfortunately, even in our churches. Sadly, too many of our conversations have become mere competitions of who knows the most. We take great satisfaction in our academic achievements, informational depth, and argumentative skills—to the point where many feel that they "know it all." Is there anything we haven't heard; anything we have yet to learn? *We* have the truth—the *full* truth! We understand the past; we even claim to have the future pretty much figured out! Is there anything left for us to know?

The Pharisees thought this way. Naturally, they were getting quite frustrated with Jesus; He has the tendency to challenge a person's "knowledge" about the things of God. The crowds were even starting to murmur that Jesus might really be the promised Messiah—and the Pharisees were positive He wasn't (or at least wouldn't admit that possibility). They had had enough of Him. So, they sent out the temple guards to arrest Jesus (see John 7:32-52). When the guards returned without Him, the chief priests and Pharisees were noticeably upset. They demanded to know why the guards failed to arrest Him. "No one ever spoke the way this man does," the guards answered.

They returned empty handed and all they could say was that Jesus was a good speaker? It was obvious that Jesus had an affect on these guards; His impact on them was strong enough that they did not seem to be concerned that they had disobeyed orders. It would appear, then, that what they were taught about Jesus was different than what they experienced. (I wonder how many times that still happens!)

It is evident that the Pharisees did not appreciate their blatant disobedience though: "'You mean he has deceived you also?' They retorted. 'Has any of the rulers or of the Pharisees believed in him? No! But this mob that knows nothing of the law—there is a curse on them'" (John 7:47–49).

Did you catch their reasoning? It was all too obvious to them that Jesus had to have deceived everyone since *they* knew better than to believe in Him. If the spiritual leaders didn't believe, it couldn't be true, right? They argued that regular people clearly didn't know the law like they did. In fact, the Pharisees said that those who actually believed in, and followed, Jesus were cursed (lit. "condemned by God"). Their "knowledge" said that Jesus couldn't be the Messiah, even though the *experience* of the guards seemed to say otherwise.

In what might appear as a half attempt to defend, Nicodemus, one of the Pharisees, spoke up. "Does our law condemn anyone without first listening to him to find out what he is doing?" His argument made sense; he was simply suggesting that they go and hear Jesus for themselves. Then they could see what He was all about. After that, Nicodemus noted, they could make their final judgment. How did his fellow Pharisees respond? "Are you from Galilee too? Look into it, and you will find that a prophet does not come out of Galilee." Once again, their "knowledge" triumphed! Who could argue with their logic? To them it was simple: Jesus couldn't be who people claimed Him to be—He was from Galilee, and no prophecy said that a prophet comes out of there.

Certainly the Pharisees and teachers of the law, who know the law and prophecies so well, would recognize when a prophecy was being fulfilled, wouldn't they? It should be easy to evaluate their track record by looking at a few of examples. So let's see how well did they did.

Matthew 2:1–8 tells the story of the visit of the Magi. As the story goes, they followed the star and found themselves eventually in Herod's court at the request of Herod himself. Herod had heard that they were looking for a king of the Jews. Of course, Herod went directly to those who would know where this king would be born: the chief priests and teachers of the law. This was an easy question for them! Of course they *knew*. The prophecies said the Messiah would be born in Bethlehem. Later that night, they were in Bethlehem worshipping Jesus with the wise men, right? Nope. The Magi from the East recognized the sign (even a pagan King seemed to), but the scholars did not! Not good for them so far.

Let's look at another story: Matthew 12:22–24. Here we find Jesus healing a demon-possessed, blind and deaf man. Those who had *seen* it wondered if He was the Messiah. Yet, the Pharisees, having only *heard* about it, said Jesus was doing it through the prince of demons. *Really?* Casual bystanders even considered that Jesus might be from God! But did the Pharisees? Nope. They missed again. Certainly, with another chance, these experts of scripture could recognize *something*.

How about the incident recorded in Matthew 17:10–13? After Peter, James, and John witnessed the transfiguration, they asked Jesus about the current leadership's teachings on the coming of Elijah. Jesus told them that Elijah would come, and had already come, but "they [the leadership] did not recognize him."

We could find many more similar stories, but I think you get the idea. Jesus even told the Pharisees in Matthew 16:3 that they did well at interpreting the appearance of the sky, but "cannot interpret the signs of the times." These spiritual leaders—religious scholars even—were actually only qualified to recognize normal changes in the weather!

How is it possible to have so much scriptural "knowledge" and still not be able to recognize God? It starts with the fact that they had the Messiah all figured out: how He would come, what He would look like, and what He would do. Since Jesus didn't fit *their* messianic predictions, they ignored Him. They said, "*We* know the Law, and he contradicts it! *We* know prophecy, and he doesn't fit it." Their "wisdom," however, was spoken of long before:

> How can you say, "We are wise, for we have the law of the LORD," when actually the lying pen of the scribe has handled it falsely? The wise will be put to shame; they will be dismayed and trapped. Since they have rejected the word of the LORD, what kind of wisdom do they have? (Jeremiah 8:8, 9)

Jesus did not fit their idea of God so they rejected Him; they rejected the Living Word! What kind of wisdom could they have?

You see, they missed the Messiah because, although they *knew* scriptures, they did not *know* God. There's a big difference. In the New Testament, there are two words in the Greek for "to know": one (*oida*) contains the idea of possessing information, and the other (*ginosko*) focuses more on the idea of knowledge gained through personal experience. (This second definition is also the meaning of the only Hebrew word translated as "know" in the Old Testament. So, every time you read the verb "know," or its variants, in the Old Testament, it is speaking of experiential knowledge, not book knowledge.)

Let me share a couple of stories that illustrate the differences of these words. In Luke 4:34, a demon confronted Jesus and said, "Go away! What do you want with us, Jesus of Nazareth? Have you come to destroy us? I know [*oida*] who you are—the Holy One of God!" The demon told Jesus that he had information on Him. Basically: I've heard of you. But then in Acts 19:15, there's another encounter with demons (this time by the seven sons of Sceva). The sons were attempting to cast out a demon "in the name of Jesus, who Paul preaches." Notice the different use of words in the demon's reply this time: "Jesus I know [*ginosko*], and I know [*oida*] about Paul, but who are you?" By the time of this story, the demons had heard of—had the information on—Paul, but they had actually *experienced* Jesus!

Sadly, the Pharisees possessed information on the scriptures but did not recognize God; they had not had a personal experience with Him. Interestingly, it was this "experiential" knowledge that Nicodemus was suggesting back in John 7. He told them that they should make a decision about Jesus only after they *experienced* Him. Nevertheless, the Pharisees were very proud of *their* wisdom. But this is what God says about their kind of wisdom:

> Let not the wise man boast of his wisdom or the strong man of his strength or the rich man of his riches, but let him who boasts boast about this: that he understands and knows me, that I am the LORD, who exercises kindness, justice and righteousness on earth, for in these I delight. (Jeremiah 9:23, 24)

Can you guess which kind of "know" God is talking about? Personal experience! God doesn't desire that we merely possess knowledge of Him—He wants us to experience Him! We like to put so much emphasis on information, but what really matters is this: have we *experienced* God?

All throughout the Bible, God invites us to this experience. Remember, the verb in the original Hebrew always expresses an experiential knowledge. This brings new meaning to verses like, "Be still and know that I am God" (Psalm 46:10), and "I will give them a heart to know me, that I am the LORD" (Jeremiah 24:7). In fact, 124 times in Ezekiel, God says that when His prophecies are fulfilled, those watching "will know that I am the LORD." The understanding of prophecy was never for the purpose of making us scholarly; we see how well the "scholars" in Jesus' day did in recognizing the true fulfillment of prophecy. No, even the ability to understand prophecy was intended to help us experience God!

This experiential knowledge is what sets the people of God apart: they recognize Him. It is why Jesus says in John 10:14, "I am the good shepherd; I know my sheep and my sheep know me." (Both times uses the word *ginosko.*) John writes in 1 John 4:8 that "Whoever does not love does not know God, because God is love." In other words, if you have experienced God you will love. God doesn't want us to simply have information about Him—so we might do better at biblical trivia—He wants us to *personally* experience Him!

You may be wondering if any of this matters? Proverbs 1:7 says, "The fear of the LORD is the beginning of knowledge." In other words, true knowledge or wisdom comes from fearing (or being in awe of) God, and how can you be in awe of Him if you have not experienced Him? But it does not work the other way around: we can possess all the information about Jesus and yet miss Him. We can memorize whole passages of scripture and still never experience God. The Pharisees' example makes it clear that a love for *our* knowledge can actually prevent us from genuinely experiencing God. What a scary thought! Think about it: they had so much information about the Messiah, yet they completely missed Him—refused to *experience* Him—while He was here.

Could you be in danger of this today? Could you be so set in your own "understanding" of scripture and prophecy yet-to-be-fulfilled that you might miss its actual fulfillment? The example of the spiritual leaders in Jesus' day reveals how dangerous it is to specify how something *might be* fulfilled because you can become so stuck on your idea that you miss the real thing!

You might be thinking, well, *they* may have been in error, but *I* have it all figured out. Really? Are you smarter than the Pharisees? Or could it be possible that you might have fallen in love with your knowledge and understanding of scripture and prophecy, yet have had no real, personal experience with God? What good is it to know the details of the Second Coming, but not know the One Who is coming? If you do not experience Him now, how will you recognize Him when He comes?

I know there's a tendency to defend your current, cherished knowledge with arguments about how you were taught in the past. I am guilty of that too. Yet, have you ever noticed how much Jesus had to re-teach the crowds sitting at His feet? While there will always be more for us to learn, there is *much* more for us to unlearn. Can you see why the Pharisees rarely sat there? They felt that they already knew all there was to know, and Jesus constantly threatened their comfort of "knowing." Unfortunately, many of them would rather be right than truly know God.

Still, those who really wanted to *know* God sat at Jesus' feet. They could tell, as He spoke, that there was something special about Him. Jesus said that He is the way and the truth and the life; He is the only way to the Father, because, "If you really knew me, you would know my Father as well" (John 14:6, 7).

The great lie Adam and Eve accepted was that humans could have knowledge outside of God. Yet, nothing could be further from the truth! To know Jesus is to know everything that is worth knowing. Jesus *is* everything. He is the way—so you follow; He is the truth—so you listen; He is the life—so you hold on.

Do you want to be smarter than a Pharisee? Then quit thinking you know it all and learn from Jesus; let Him re-teach you. Empty yourself of the things you imagine you "know" and sit at *His feet* and listen—*experience Him*—and know Him.

"Now this is eternal life: that they *know* you, the only true God, and Jesus Christ, whom you sent" (John 17:3, emphasis mine).

Chapter Five

"Here I am! I stand at the door and knock.
If anyone hears my voice and opens the door,
I will come in and eat with him, and he with me."
– REVELATION 3:20

Hangin' with the Holiest

It is said that birds of a feather flock together. For the most part, it is hard to argue with this. It's true that people who have similar beliefs or passions are often drawn together. We see it everywhere. Some of these flocks are labeled cliques, some clans; some may be called secret societies, or political parties, or denominations. Whatever it may be called, the idea is definitely taught early. Many of us are warned as children to be careful of whom we hang around. The thought goes: if birds of a feather flock together and you are seen with that "flock," people will assume you are the same "bird" as the flock. Or, to avoid being associated with "bad apples," don't spend any time with those "apples." Sounds simple enough.

Of course, we Christians usually tack on another warning: those we spend time with can have an influence on us—and they may actually *change* us! While this can often be true, and should be a reason for careful consideration when choosing those you spend the most time with, it doesn't seem to concern us as much as it should. Rather, we frequently come across as being more concerned about appearances. Thus, our favorite default phrase: *"avoid the appearance of evil."* Notice, it is not avoiding evil, but avoiding the "appearance" of evil. This thinking can actually be dangerous to ministry: it states that if you are *seen* with someone who is not a Christian, people may *conclude* that you are not a Christian either. Therefore, be careful of those you are *seen* with. As a result, you may simply steer clear of anyone who isn't just like you (or who you think you are) and that way you can't be wrongly associated with them. But many think it doesn't matter with whom you choose to spend your time, as long as no other church members find out about it!

We have already discovered that the Pharisees did nearly everything for the sake of being seen by others. So it is no stretch of the imagination to witness them being also concerned about those with whom they are seen. They went through much trouble to make sure that the groups they hung around made them look good. This way, when people saw them hanging out with the "holiest" of the church, that perceived holiness would also be accredited to them. This is like saying that spending time with athletes makes you look more athletic (I wish!). It is easy, then, to understand why they couldn't figure out Jesus. He was so radical in His thinking. He not only taught sinners, which obviously *someone* has to do, but He even ate with them!

The first time such an odd dinner engagement is recorded is when Jesus ate at Levi's (Matthew's) house, just after calling him to be a disciple. During the meal, several tax collectors and sinners also arrived to eat with them. Noticing this, the Pharisees become uncomfortable and asked the disciples a question that many would continue to ask throughout Jesus' ministry: "Why does He eat with tax collectors and sinners?" (Mark 2:16). Did Jesus not realize what this might do to His reputation? How could He allow

Himself to be seen with such . . . *trash?* What kind of person would hang out with sinners?

Jesus overheard the inquiry and answered it Himself: "It is not the healthy who need a doctor, but the sick. I have not come to call the righteous, but sinners" (Mark 2:17). In other words, Jesus was basically saying, "I *have* to be here. This is *why* I came! *This* is my ministry."

Okay. So Jesus' ministry was to eat with sinners. So it went against the cultural norm. But, why would He do it? It was obvious to the Pharisees that Jesus couldn't be *that* righteous considering that the people they saw Him with were sinners. Yet, what good could come from eating with them? Why was it so crucial to Jesus that He would risk His reputation?

Another story explains His reasons well. It is recorded in Luke 19. According to chapter 18, Jesus and His disciples were heading to Jerusalem for the Passover (His last one). Their journey would take them right through Jericho. Chapter 19 begins with Jesus making His way through the city. As He was passing through, we are introduced to a certain man: Zacchaeus.

Zacchaeus is not introduced in a flattering way. He is revealed as a chief tax collector—in other words, the head of the most hated group in Israel. Tax collectors were considered the lowest a person could get in society. Rome had learned that it could get consistent taxes by having locals collecting from their own people. How the locals did it Rome didn't care, as long as they got paid. Unfortunately, the tax collectors became known for cheating the people and demanding high penalties from them. As a result, some of them would get rich—another condemning description of Zacchaeus. There was no question how he obtained his money. He was swindling his own people. This guy was as low as a person could get—a traitor—the chief scum of his day.

Still, somehow he found out about Jesus and the Bible says that he wanted to see Him. Maybe he simply wanted to put a face with a name. It doesn't mention anything about him wanting to actually meet Jesus, just that he wanted to see Him. He was likely used to the fact that someone like Jesus would never spend time with someone like him. The Pharisees certainly wouldn't. But it didn't matter. When he got to the road he couldn't see anyway—the crowd was too large and too tall for him to see Jesus. Zacchaeus was actually too short (the Greek word here literally means "*micro*"). What a reason! He literally *was* the lowest in society!

Yet, crafty man that he was, he ran ahead of the crowd and found a high spot—which just happened to be a tree—and climbed up. Then he waited. Jesus was traveling on the road that went through Jericho, and this tree was right by that road. He had to pass by and then Zacchaeus would surely get to see, regardless of the crowd.

His waiting paid off. Jesus did arrive, but there was a surprise: He didn't simply pass by. He stopped. He stopped right under the tree. Can you image Zacchaeus' shock and excitement? Then Jesus spoke directly to him. What an amazing turn of events! This was *way* more than he ever could have imagined. Stopping the whole procession, Jesus looked up into the tree and invited Zacchaeus to come down. And this was the reason why: "I must stay at your house today." He *must*?

Now, we could understand Jesus saying, "I'd like to go to your house sometime." Or, "Would you mind if I stopped at your house for some tea today?" But Jesus said that it was absolutely necessary that He stay at his house, *today!* It had to be today! (Of course, Jesus *was* on His way to Jerusalem to be *crucified*. If He was going to spend time with Zacchaeus it *had* to be that day.) It didn't matter why to Zacchaeus; he quickly climbed down and welcomed Jesus into his home, rejoicing. What a happy day for Zacchaeus! Can you imagine? All he intended was to see Jesus—maybe shake His hand or get an autograph—but now Jesus was actually sitting at *his* table, eating *his* food.

Not everyone was so happy though. Verse 7 says that some who saw this began to mutter, "He has gone to be the guest of a 'sinner.'" You might have seen their heads shaking as they spoke. It appears that this group shared the ideology of the Pharisees. By their mumblings, they obviously thought they would have been the better choice. Jesus would have been smarter to go to one of *their* homes, not *this* sinner's. Surely Jesus could do better! This was a no brainer for them: Zacchaeus was a chief tax collector. No one who ever considered themselves a good Israelite would be caught dead with such a man, let alone *eat* with him! Yet, Jesus, the rumored Messiah, was not only eating with him, but lodging with him too? What kind of person would hang out with scum like that? A special kind of person, that's who. Consider the effect Jesus has on His host: "But Zacchaeus stood up and said to the Lord, 'Look, Lord! Here and now I give half of my possessions to the poor, and if I have cheated anybody out of anything, I will pay back four times the amount'" (Luke 19:8).

This was coming from the chief cheater? He had a complete change of heart? Full repentance after just one meal? I'm not sure they were even finished with that one meal. Zacchaeus didn't even know what Jesus looked like before that day, and then suddenly he was willing to change his whole life. That must have been *some* meal, right? No. That is *Jesus*. Then Jesus made this statement: "Today salvation has come to this house, because this man, too, is a son of Abraham. For the Son of Man came to seek and save the lost" (Luke 19:9, 10). That is why it was necessary for Jesus to come *today*—because *today* salvation came. Salvation cannot wait until tomorrow. For all of heaven's occupants, saving mankind is always urgent.

Can you imagine the joy in Zacchaeus' house that evening? Can you imagine the celebration in heaven when this lost son was found? It was for this reason that Jesus came. It is why He went to Zacchaeus' house *that* day. It is why He was willing to hang with sinners: because He knew that when He spent time with someone, He could have an influence on them.

You see, we have grown so worried about the influence people may have on us that we never think about the influence we may have on them. The Pharisees only spent time with people who made them look good and feel good about themselves. But Jesus went to the people He could have an eternal influence on, not those who thought they were already good enough. So, who do you resemble more when you choose your friends? Do you only hang out with those who will make you look good and feel good about yourself? Or, do you hang out with those you can bless by introducing them to the gospel that is Jesus? Who do you have an influence on?

I know it's not easy to spend time with the down-and-out. It's not easy having lunch with the guy that stinks, or making friends with the girl who is always quietly sitting in the corner, or talking with that person who is just plain weird. Yet, what if today Jesus was going to bring salvation to that person, because you brought Jesus to that person today? Salvation doesn't wait for tomorrow, because tomorrow could be too late!

Of course, before we can be capable of leading someone to Jesus, we need to have a Zacchaeus experience ourselves, which is something, sadly, most Pharisees never do. You see, we are all Zacchaeus—all sinners needing a savior and possibly not even knowing it. In Revelation 3, Jesus tells us our condition:

> I know your deeds, that you are neither cold nor hot. I wish that you were either one or the other! So, because you are lukewarm—neither hot nor cold—I am about to spit you out of my mouth. You say, "I am rich; I have acquired wealth and do not need a thing." But you do not realize that you are wretched, poor, blind and naked. (Verses 15–17)

Zacchaeus thought he was rich until he met Jesus and found out what true riches were. Similarly, the Pharisees thought they were spiritually rich. They thought they didn't need anything. Just like Laodicea (more on this group in chapter 16). Just like many of us. We think we are spiritually rich. We often think we are the best history has to offer. We frequently think we have everything we need. But this couldn't be further from the truth. Yet, if we will listen, Jesus has a recommendation:

I counsel you to buy from me gold refined in the fire, so you can become rich; and white clothes to wear, so you can cover your shameful nakedness; and salve to put on your eyes, so you can see. Those whom I love I rebuke and discipline. So be earnest, and repent. Here I am! I stand at the door and knock. If anyone hears my voice and opens the door, *I will come in and eat with him, and he with me.* (Revelation 3:18–20, emphasis mine)

Friend, this is it! This is your sycamore tree moment! This is your chance to hang out with *the* Holiest! Today, Jesus wants to come to your house! He's knocking on your door. He says if you open the door—if you earnestly come down from your "high place" and accept Him as guest—He'll come in and *eat with you!*

Jesus is still very active in His ministry. He is still eating with sinners; He is still bringing salvation to households. Oddly, the Pharisees, who taught the great importance of wisely choosing the crowd with whom you spent time, didn't spend time with Jesus. They perfected avoiding those who would hurt their holy-façade, even when it meant avoiding the One who could make them truly holy. Do not make the same mistake!

Can you hear Him? He is still going door to door knocking on the hearts of us all. How wonderful would it be to hear these words spoken of you: *"today salvation has come into this house"*? It is crucial that Jesus comes into your life today. Salvation cannot wait until tomorrow. Don't wait! Open the door. Let Him in. Eat with Him. If you are not sure what it means to let Him into your life, think about what it meant for Zacchaeus. It means that you let Jesus influence you, change you, and clean up your life. It means *listening* to Him. It means making Him your CEO, not your partner. So, accept Him in as your guest *today.* Take time to hang with the Holiest so that *today* salvation may come to your house!

Chapter Six

"But mark this: There will be terrible times in the last days.
People will be lovers of themselves, lovers of money, boastful,
proud, abusive, disobedient to their parents, ungrateful, unholy,
without love, unforgiving, slanderous, without self-control,
brutal, not lovers of the good, treacherous, rash, conceited,
lovers of pleasure rather than lovers of God—
having a form of godliness but denying its power.
Have nothing to do with them."
— 2 TIMOTHY 3:1–5

The Oldest Profession

For as long as I can remember I have loved wearing costumes. The idea of dressing up and "becoming" someone else has always fascinated me. So it would not be much of a surprise to learn that, when I was a child, one of my favorite times of the year was Halloween. It wasn't for the bag of candy (although I never complained!)—and it definitely wasn't for the scary things usually associated with the holiday—it was for the costumes. I could *be* someone else. I've been through all sorts of costumes: homemade, cheap store-bought, fancy store-bought, and partial. I didn't really care for the partials. Partials were when you didn't have a whole costume and you had to combine a few just to make one.

One year I desperately wanted to go as C-3PO (the gold robot from Star Wars), but for some reason or another I didn't have the complete costume. All I had was the hard plastic facemask that was only held on by a thin, cut-your-ears-tough, rubber band. Disappointed, and unwilling to go as anything else (the only other available option that year was my sister's hand-me-down princess costume), I was given a compromise: my C-3PO mask with . . . Fred Flintstone clothes. They were not even the nice ones. These were pullover, printed-on-a-plastic-bag Fred Flintstone clothes. I was a character mess! I was sci-fi and Stone Age at the same time. At the doors, when asked who I was supposed to be, I didn't really know what to say.

But my time came eventually. Years later, I was able to wear a pretty nice Superman costume. It even came with a cape! I didn't have the slicked black hair—or the bulging super muscles for that matter—but I felt special. There was no question about who I was. For that brief moment, I even felt a little like Superman. And why not? With the costume on I sort of looked like Superman. So I ran everywhere proclaiming what was outwardly obvious to me: *I am Superman!* The more I shouted this statement, the more I believed it. So I took the next natural step (at least to me): I tried to fly. No, I didn't jump from the roof or anything like that. I just tried to jump off our front porch, but guess what? I didn't fly. That day I learned that I could look and claim the part but it did no good without the power. Although I professed to be super, I couldn't back it up with any evidence.

This is the oldest profession. (Did you think this was going to be about something else?) Truly, the oldest *profession* in the world is claiming to be something that you are not.

Consider Cain and Abel. Cain and Abel both offered sacrifices to God—yet God only accepted Abel's. At first glance, it is hard for us to tell the difference between the two offerings, besides what was being offered. We may even side with Cain on this. It doesn't seem fair. Cain *does* appear to be doing the right thing. He offered a sacrifice just as God asked. So, how could God turn him down? Cain professed to be giving an offering to God and visibly gave the offering, yet something was missing.

We have already learned that the Pharisees were the self-proclaimed holy ones of their day. They did not start with this self-proclamation, but after being observed for a while, other people labeled them as the example of holiness. Sometimes people are given titles they don't live up to. And even though they didn't live up to the label, they began to like it and eventually held onto it. By this time, nearly everyone *believed* the Pharisees were the prime example of godly living. They claimed to be obedient to God's law and everyone saw how strict they were with the Sabbath and other biblical laws. Their claims seemed to be backed up with evidence. It would appear that they had the right to claim such godliness. Yet, Jesus would disagree. Listen to what He said:

> Woe to you, teachers of the law and Pharisees, you hypocrites! You are like whitewashed tombs, which look clean on the outside but on the inside are full of dead men's bones and everything unclean. In the same way, on the outside you appear to people as righteous but on the inside you are full of hypocrisy and wickedness. (Matthew 23:27, 28)

Ouch! The Jews were accustomed to whitewashing a tomb's entrance (especially those that were in caves) as a warning against defilement, which would be caused by entering or even touching the tombs. Things were also whitewashed to hide what was really there. So basically, Jesus was saying, "You guys look spiffy but you really stink. You *look* godly, but you are trying to cover up all that wickedness."

The Pharisees, according to Jesus, were trying to hide who they really were. They were a warning to others. They professed to be living for God, but instead they were spiritually dead. They professed to be godly, and possibly even *looked* godly, but were actually full of wickedness. Their claims of godliness may have been fulfilled in man's sight, but not in God's.

I wish I could say that this spirit of the Pharisees does not continue to our time, but it does. Paul warns us about it:

> But mark this: There will be terrible times in the last days. People will be lovers of themselves, lovers of money, boastful, proud, abusive, disobedient to their parents, ungrateful, unholy, without love, unforgiving, slanderous, without self-control, brutal, not lovers of the good, treacherous, rash, conceited, lovers of pleasure rather than lovers of God—having a form of godliness but denying its power. Have nothing to do with them. (2 Timothy 3:1–5)

This is not a pretty picture. Paul is talking about the last days; the days in which we are living. Naturally, we may think of a bad neighborhood in a major city. Yet the description he gives is not of the attitude of the general world population, but of those who *claim godliness*. As horrible as it is, Paul is talking about many Christians today. A group of end-time Pharisees—in full costume. They have an "outward form" of godliness. They look the part. They profess to be God-like, but their lives *deny His power*.

What catches my attention in this text is that Paul is asserting that true godly people *should* be experiencing this power! It was something Jesus had promised: "I am going to send you what my Father has promised; but stay in the city until you have been clothed with power from on high" (Luke 24:49). What a beautiful thought! Clothed, wrapped up all snug and cozy, in God's power. He tells us in Acts 1:8 that this power would come, "when the Holy Spirit comes on you."

According to Jesus, we receive this power when the Holy Spirit comes *on* us. It can also mean coming upon and overtaking. In other words, when the Holy Spirit comes and takes over, we receive power. And not just any power: the Greek word translated as "power" in Acts 1:8 is *dunamis*, from which we get our English words *dynamite* or *dynamic*. What is dynamite like? It's explosive. It's destructive. It's aggressive. It moves, alters, and renews. This is a power that can completely demolish obstacles and remove walls. It's a power that changes things. It's a power that can only come from God. The power He has promised to give us.

So the disciples obeyed Jesus and waited for the Holy Spirit before starting their work. How sad that so often today we rush ahead of God, doing "His work," but not waiting for the Holy Spirit. No wonder we find ourselves burned-out and powerless. But what happens when you wait for the Holy Spirit to come upon you? Pentecost! Thousands reached for the kingdom of God in *one day*! This is the power of God. This power is promised to each one of His followers. So, what has happened? Where is this power? According to the Bible, this power should be still evident in our lives.

I must confess that I still struggle with what Jesus said in John 14:12. He said, "I tell you the truth, anyone who has faith in me will do what I have been doing. He will do even greater things than these because I am going to the Father." I struggle with this because it seems so impossible. It is easy to apply this promise to the disciples sitting before Jesus that day but not to all disciples till the end. Sure, they did great things in the name of Jesus, but that was *then*. Things like that don't happen anymore, do they? *Why not?* They should! Jesus never said He would stop giving us power. Actually, Jesus said *anyone* who has faith in Him would do *greater* things because He was going to His Father. He promised us power through the Holy Spirit to accomplish it.

Yet today, we often only experience a "pretty" outward form of godliness, but no power. We claim to be Christians. We wear Christian clothes, drive Christian cars, and even eat Christian food. To just about anyone, we look the part. We even start feeling it. Yet the reality of our lives denies the power of God. It reminds me of a poster I saw on a bulletin board in my dorm lobby during college: "*If you were arrested for being a Christian, would there be enough evidence to convict you?*"

The Pharisees tried to cover up their wickedness with white-washed living. They did not understand what the power of God could have done in their lives, so they remained spiritually dead, and missed out. They were only pretty tombs. Would you want Jesus to describe you this way? God forbid!

You cannot try to cover up your sins and still expect to see His power in your life. So, quit trying. God doesn't want you to hide behind a whitewashed wall. He doesn't want you to pretend to live; He wants you to abundantly live. He doesn't want you to have a form of godliness; He wants you to *be* godly. God wants to give you power through the Holy Spirit. Power to uproot the deepest sins, overcome the greatest obstacles, and remove the Devil's strongholds. Power to change lives.

You may already experience this power in your life. If so, praise the Lord! May He continue to do amazing things through you. But, maybe your Christian life is currently powerless. Would you like a godly life, full of power? Peter says in Acts 2:38, "Repent and be baptized, everyone of you, in the name of Jesus Christ for the forgiveness of your sins. And you will receive the gift of the Holy Spirit." If you want the Holy Spirit in your life, the first thing you need to do is repent. Repent means to turn around or, as the Old Testament says it, return to God. The next thing you must do is follow Him. This is the essence of what baptism means—the public declaration of your discipleship to Jesus. When you follow Jesus, you take the student position: He is your leader, teacher, and master. You get your direction and counsel for life from Him. According to the Bible, it is when you are in this relationship with Jesus and fully following His leading that the gift and the power of the Spirit will come upon you.

You may be thinking, "I've done this already, but I don't see God's power in my life." Is it possible that you might have repented at one point in your life and, since then, have walked away from depending on God? It's an unfortunate human trait. But the good news is that if at any point you realize that you have walked away from God, you need only to *return*. If you find your spiritual life powerless, there can only be one reason why—you have somehow wandered away from God. If you want the power of God in our life, *you must have* God *in your life!*

People may tell you that these miraculous acts spoken of in the Bible regarding this power cannot happen in our day; they may claim it's impossible. It's time for this thinking to change because God never changes! If He says that His people, even in these last days, will be filled with His power that can change lives around them, then it is true. So, why live a pretend life when God promises to give you a power-filled life? Put your complete dependence on Christ—follow Him—that your life may be full of the power of the Holy Spirit!

Chapter Seven

"Jesus replied, 'I tell you the truth, everyone who sins is
a slave to sin. Now a slave has no permanent place in
the family, but a son belongs to it forever. So if the Son
sets you free, you will be free indeed.'"

– JOHN 8:34–36

The Fantastic Freedom Fighters

What is freedom to you? For many it comes down to the ability to make choices. Whatever freedom is to you, would you say that it is worth fighting for? What would you do if you lost it? Right now, we live in the "land of the free." But, what would you say if I told you that it was all a lie—that you weren't ever really free? You might be as surprised to hear that as the Israelites were.

Of course, no one would deny that slavery was a significant part of Israel's history. Freedom was an off and on experience for them. Starting with the famous exodus from slavery in Egypt by Moses, their history is filled with moments when men and women rise to fight for their freedom. This was also true during the Maccabean wars, which were fought during the time between when the last Old Testament book was written and Jesus' birth. Israel was facing the loss of freedom once again. It was during these wars that a fairly new group rose up and fought hard for their nation's freedom: we know them as the Pharisees. They were fantastic! Many Pharisees gave up their lives to ensure Israel's freedom. And these fantastic freedom fighters succeeded: Israel had been "free" from that point on. So it is no wonder that they were surprised to hear Jesus talk of setting them free:

> To the Jews who had believed him, Jesus said, "If you hold to my teachings, then you are really my disciples. Then you will know the truth, and the truth will set you free." They answered him, "we are Abraham's descendants and have never been slaves to anyone. How can you say that we shall be set free?" (John 8:31–33)

What could He be talking about? They *were* free! They had good ol' Hebrew pride. "We've *never* been slaves," they argued. The Pharisees had seen to it that Israel was free. So, in their lifetime, they had only known freedom. At least they *felt* free. They were free, weren't they? They had to be. That's what they had been told. If they weren't free, what happened?

You see, there's an inevitable issue with freedom: true freedom allows for choices—both the good and the bad. Consider Adam and Eve: they were created with true freedom. You might suggest that they had rules too. It is true that God said they could eat from any tree in the garden, with the exception of one specific tree in the middle—the tree of Knowledge of Good and Evil.

It is interesting when you consider what God was asking them to avoid. As we learned earlier, in the Old Testament, "knowledge" was obtained by experience. This is the basic idea in the Hebrew word for "knowledge." With this understanding, we can see that God forbidding them to eat from the tree was about wanting them to avoid an experience. So, what had Adam and Eve experienced up to this point? Only good. Then all God really asked them to do was to stay away from the tree that would give them the experience of evil. Not such a bad rule, is it?

Another interesting side of this story is that both the Tree of Life and the Tree of Knowledge of Good and Evil were in the middle of the garden. So, this means that every time they entered the center of the garden they could choose either eternal life or the experience of evil.

Yes, they had to choose, but *they had the choice.* God allowed them to choose either way. Were they able to eat from *every* tree, even the one God asked them to avoid? Absolutely. They were physically able, *and* had the freedom to choose either way. Of course, just because they had the freedom to choose, doesn't mean that both choices were good. The rule was provided to show what was best for them. By ignoring God's "rule" they chose the worst for themselves.

This is what made the Pharisees eventually uncomfortable with freedom. It was evident to them that free people don't always make the right choice; the years of wars and history of slavery was enough proof. If they kept the people from making the wrong choices, the nation wouldn't suffer. So, in an effort to keep the people free from bad choices, they took their choice away. God counseled the people on what to do; the Pharisees forced them. God gave a principle; the Pharisees applied it for them. *They* made the choices for Israel. In the eyes of the Pharisees, it was worth sacrificing some of the freedom of the people—by removing their choice—if they could prevent them from angering God. So, the group who once fought hard for the freedom of Israel eventually became the group who fought zealously against it. Jesus calls them out on it in Matthew 23:

> Woe to you, teachers of the law and Pharisees, you hypocrites! You shut the kingdom of heaven in man's faces. You yourselves do not enter, nor will you let those enter who are trying to. . . . Woe to you, teachers of the law and Pharisees, you hypocrites! You travel over land and sea to win a single convert, and when he becomes one, you make him twice as much a son of hell as you are. (Verses 13, 15)

How could they "shut the kingdom of heaven in men's faces"? If the kingdom of heaven is a free gift that a person must choose to accept, then the only way to shut someone out is to remove a person's ability, or right, to choose it. This is exactly what the Pharisees did. By creating rules that had to be obeyed, they sent Israel back into slavery. Israel wasn't free to serve God; they were really just slaves to the many standards of the Pharisees. And by following the Pharisees, instead of following God, they would end up just as wicked (if not more). So, although Israel was politically free, they were spiritual slaves.

I wish I could say that we are safe from this happening today but, once again, we are not. We too are in danger of losing our freedom. In fact, we may have already lost it! Some proclaim that one day the government may take away our freedom. But what if it has already been taken away? Consider this: does the structure of your "Christianity" support your freedom to choose, or does it tend to make choices for you? What about your church? Maybe you're not as free as you think.

Jesus said He would set Israel free and explained why to the confused crowd. He said that everyone who sins is a slave to sin. And if you are a slave to anything, you are not part of the family like a son is. However, "if the Son sets you free, you will be free indeed" (John 8:34–36).

If you get anything from this chapter, I hope it is this: *unless Jesus sets you free, you are not free.* You cannot be freed by a church. You cannot be freed by doctrines. You cannot be freed by a pastor. No matter how good those things may be, *only Jesus can truly set you free.* Why? It is because He's the One who originally created us to be free. Once sin entered humanity, that freedom was taken away. As it is, you really have no choices under sin; there is only one outcome, one path. But when Jesus enters your life, He restores your choices. The One who originally entrusted mankind with freedom is the only one who can truly restore it.

He not only gives you freedom, but has fought hard for it too. Freedom always comes at a cost. Revelation 1:5 says that He "has freed us from our sins by his blood." This is why we often say, "Jesus paid the price." He gave His life in the fight to restore your freedom. Praise the Lord! Romans 8:1, 2 tells us how this is all possible: "Therefore, there is now no condemnation for those who are in Christ Jesus, because through Christ Jesus the law of the Spirit of life set me free from the law of sin and death."

According to Jesus, there is a "new" law given to us through the Spirit. This is not a law we are used to—a law that binds us and takes away our choices—but this is a law that frees us and restores our choices. It is a law that is *directing* our choices rather than *making* them. This is the freedom Jesus fought for. This is the freedom He paid for. This is the freedom you can have!

Now, I must warn you. Satan will try to take it away from you every chance he gets. Therefore we must heed Paul's warning—"It is for freedom that Christ has set us free. Stand firm, then, and do not let yourselves be burdened again by the yoke of slavery" (Galatians 5:1). You may wonder how this could happen? 1 Corinthians 7:23 says, "You were bought at a price; do not become the slaves of men." In other words, once you choose to follow God, *follow God*. Period. No one else is worthy to follow. This means that no one else should direct your path. No one can tell you what you can do or can't do. Other people do not have the authority to tell you what to eat or drink or wear, or how to worship—unless you *give* them the authority. If you claim to follow God, then listen to *Him*. When He counsels you in what to eat or drink or how to worship, then you listen to *His* counsel.

Does this mean that you beat up anyone who might try to teach you? No, of course not! It means you must check *everything* out for yourself with God, in His Word and with prayer, before you accept any teaching—*before* you follow. God often uses people to teach us, but we still only follow God. We don't want to follow someone else blindly, no matter how nice they may be, because following blindly is still slavery.

I will guess that there are a few who might be squirming right now at the thought of rampant freedom. Some of you are thinking,

"Bah Humbug! This can only result in chaos! If we let people choose, they will make the wrong choice! That can't be good for the church." Others of you may be thinking, "Woo-hoo! Freedom to do what ever I want? Adultery, here I come!"

First, to those who are worried, let me clarify by asking this question: whose choices are you ultimately accountable for? Where in the Bible does it say that you were put in charge of protecting the pure image of your denomination? The Bible says that you are to "continue to work out your salvation with fear and trembling" (Philippians 2:12). You are responsible for your own choices first. If you were to spend more time examining how your own choices reflect God, you may not even have time to worry about how someone else's choice may further tarnish an already imperfect group of God-followers.

Second, to those who are drooling: although you have the freedom to choose anything, is everything worth choosing? What does the Bible say about this? "You, my brothers, were called to be free. But do not use your freedom to indulge the sinful nature; rather, serve one another in love" (Galatians 5:13). Peter says it this way: "Live as free men, but do not use your freedom as a cover-up for evil; live as servants of God" (1 Peter 2:16). Freedom is not a license to be immoral. Just because freedom gives you the choice doesn't mean both choices will be good. Not everything you may choose from will lead to good things. You have the freedom to break the speed limit, but it doesn't mean you should. You may be able to commit adultery, but it won't strengthen your marriage (or your relationship with God)!

This is what it all comes down to: when you are a slave to sin, righteousness has no control in your life. But what good has that kind of life done for you—those things you hope nobody ever finds out about? Those things only draw you away from God. But when you are set free by Christ and begin serving Him, the result is a godlier life and eternity to look forward to. Romans 6:23 says, "For the wages of sin is death, but the gift of God is eternal life in Christ Jesus our Lord."

Is it possible that you might make a bad choice as a free person? Definitely. Unfortunately, human beings have a special talent for making bad choices. But this freedom in Christ gives you the *ability* to also make righteous choices—choices that lead to holiness, not shame; choices that lead to life, not death. The restoration of your freedom returns you to the center of the Garden of Eden to face the same choice as humanity's first parents: slavery and death in sin, or freedom and life in Jesus. Which will you choose?

A Pharisee will always take away the freedom of the people around them and make their choices for them. They will decide what others should do to please God and what to avoid doing to keep from angering Him.

Jesus came to restore your ability to choose. He has revealed the results of following His guidance in your life. He came to truly set you free. Of course, freedom does not guarantee that you will make all the right decisions. It just guarantees the right to make decisions. Satan had stolen this away from you. But, praise the Lord, Jesus paid the price for *you!* He fought for your freedom and won the true freedom that no one can take away because when "the Son sets you free, you are free indeed!" (John 8:36)

Friend, won't you accept His payment on your behalf, so you can be truly free and follow Him?

Chapter Eight

"Jews demand signs and Greeks look for wisdom, but we preach Christ crucified: a stumbling block to Jews and foolishness to Gentiles, but to those whom God has called, both Jews and Greeks, Christ the power of God and the wisdom of God."

— 1 CORINTHIANS 1:22–24

Blinded by Sight

I felt victorious as I walked out of his office. I had just finished my yearly vision test at the eye doctor. I felt proud that I was able to correctly guess which (nearly identical) testing lens was clearer—one or two? I'll admit that I was often guessing, since many times I couldn't tell any difference between one or two! Yet, that day I also felt an increase in confidence as I had successfully endured the torturous contraption that shot a "puff" of air at my eye (which, of course, should have given me greater ability to keep my eyes open during high winds). It all added up to the highly anticipated announcement of my visit: I had perfect vision. I held my shoulders a bit higher as I began to leave the building—and walked right into the window at the entrance. Yep. I missed the glass door completely and walked straight into the very clean, full-length window beside it. It was no surprise when the doctor suggested I might want to be re-checked!

As embarrassing as that was, I know I'm not the only one to have missed seeing what was right in front of me. Pharisees often suffer from this problem too, only spiritually—missing the things of God that are right in front of them. Actually, in their case, it might be more like refusing to see what is right in front of them.

The following story (found in John 9) is a prime example. Jesus was walking in Jerusalem when He found a man who was born blind. Showing compassion for the blind man, He spit on the ground, made mud and put it on the man's eyes (which certainly sounds a little unorthodox). Then He told the man to wash in the Pool of Siloam. The blind man did as he was told and came back *with sight.*

It is not long before he was recognized as the man who was supposed to be blind. People were amazed. Could this be the same man? Naturally, questions followed. He described to them about Jesus and how he followed His instructions. He was soon brought before the Pharisees, who had their own questions for him. Whether they let him completely answer their questions or not, we don't know, but it is clear from the story they didn't believe him. Something didn't seem right about his story. Their reason for doubt was that Jesus allegedly "healed" him on the Sabbath and no man of God would have done that (John 9:16).

They began to suspect trickery. Could this whole thing have been a hoax? Maybe this man wasn't blind to begin with. Yes, this wasn't a real healing after all—it was staged! So they called in his parents and questioned them. His parents verified that he was their son who was born blind, but they didn't know how he received sight. It is possible that they had an idea how, but being afraid of the spiritual leaders, they just passed the question on by saying, "Ask our son, he's a big boy. He can answer for himself."

So the Pharisees summoned the former blind man again. "Don't give credit to this sinner but to God," they demand.

The man replied, "I have no idea whether or not He is a sinner. All I know is that I used to be blind, but now I'm not!"

"Then how did he do it?" They interrogated.

Whether the man was trying to be sarcastic or was actually serious, he definitely got a reaction from his reply: "I've already told you my story and you didn't listen. Why do you keep asking about Him? Do you want to follow Him too?"

The room exploded in insults. How dare this man suggest such a thing! They were disciples of Moses and proud of it! (Hmm. That certainly revealed something about them.) Why would *they* follow this Jesus? They didn't even know from where He came.

The man was amazed at this. They didn't know where Jesus was from, yet He did something rarely, if ever, heard of before. He opened the eyes of a man born blind. "If this man were not from God, He could do nothing" (John 9:33), he stated. Unable to stand his disrespect for them any longer, they cast him out of the temple.

I find it fascinating that this "uneducated," ordinary man knew from where Jesus came while the "educated," elite Pharisees did not. One who was once blind could see that Jesus was sent from God, yet those claiming to have great spiritual insight could not. How could this be?

Jesus confirmed the existence of this condition in John 9:39 when He said that He came to the world so that "the blind would see and those who see would become blind." Upon hearing this, the Pharisees take it personally (rightly so). "Are you saying that we are blind?" They asked. Jesus replied, "If you were blind, you would not be guilty of sin; but now that you claim to see, your guilt remains" (John 9:41).

Jesus wasn't being hard on them because they had difficulty seeing; He was hard on them because in their "blindness" they claimed to be able to see. The Pharisees professed to have a greater understanding and spiritual insight than the average person. It was their arrogance in their self-proclaimed ability to recognize the things of God that Jesus condemned. But, we've already seen their recognition "ability" on display—at Jesus' birth and through-out His ministry—and it wasn't especially accurate. It is not at all surprising that they were constantly asking Him for signs. Their spiritual recognition software was especially buggy. Yet, every one of their requests for Jesus to prove Himself only demonstrated their spiritual blindness more.

Interestingly, Jesus met each request for a sign with rejection. Do not misunderstand. Jesus did many great miracles and signs, and many believed as a result. However His ministry was not about doing miracles on demand. When asked, He most often refused. Just like the time they requested a sign in Matthew 16:

> The Pharisees and Sadducees came to Jesus and tested him by asking him to show them a sign from heaven. He replied, "When evening comes, you say, 'It will be fair weather, for the sky is red,' and in the morning, 'Today it will be stormy, for the sky is red and overcast.' You know how to interpret the appearance of the sky, but you cannot interpret the signs of the times. A wicked and adulterous generation looks for a miraculous sign, but none will be given it except the sign of Jonah." Jesus then left them and went away. (Verses 1–4)

They asked for a miraculous sign and how did He respond? He calls them a wicked and adulterous generation, says no, and then walks away. Talk about rejection. This makes Jesus sound mean. They were only asking for a sign—just a little miracle—so they could believe too, right? Hardly. Mark 8:11 says that they asked Him for a sign to test Him. (Sounds like a test Jesus had in the wilderness. It stinks of the same author.) No, they didn't want a sign so they could cast away doubt from their minds and place their belief in Him as their Savior, they wanted to trap Him and cause Him to stumble.

It wasn't as if they hadn't seen a sign before. His miracles were so well-known in the area that even Herod had heard of them and was hoping to see them (Luke 23:8). One of the Pharisees' own, Nicodemus, was convinced about Jesus because of the signs he had seen. Meeting with Jesus under the cover of night he said, "Rabbi, we know you are a teacher who has come from God. For no one could perform the miraculous signs you are doing if God were not with him" (John 2:2). He admitted that this was not just known to him for he said, "*we* know." They all had noticed. That kind of thing cannot go unnoticed for long.

Yet noticing isn't everything. How they reacted to the signs made the difference. Nicodemus, and others like him, came to Christ wanting to learn more. Their reaction was to draw closer. This was not so with all of the Pharisees. Many would soon be found huddled in a room scheming to get rid of Jesus. It wouldn't be because they did not see any signs. Notice their argument: "What are we accomplishing? Here is this man performing many miraculous signs. If we let him go on like this, everyone will believe in him, and then the Romans will come and take away both our place and our nation" (John 11:47, 48).

How amazing and sad is this? They noticed Jesus' miracles and even acknowledge that His miracles would only cause more people to believe in Him, yet *they* still didn't want to believe! It wasn't as if they had only heard about it. Scripture reveals that "even after Jesus had done all these miraculous signs *in their presence*, they still would not believe in him" (John 12:37, emphasis mine). They didn't want to see a sign so they could confirm the rumors and fall at His feet to worship the One sent by God to save the world. They wanted to take Him down so they could keep their influence.

How exactly they thought this would work, I can't imagine, but Jesus never played along with their games. He usually told them they wouldn't get a sign. Not the sign they wanted, at least. Instead, Jesus only spoke of this cryptic "sign of Jonah." Surely those trained in the study of scripture could demystify a simple puzzle like this one, right?

I wonder if they developed study committees to uncover the truth about this "sign of Jonah." They might have called together the brightest minds of the most renowned teachers in an attempt to solve it. Maybe they convened at the Decoding Jonah Summit featuring all the greatest scholars of their time.

Of course, if they had actually listened to Jesus, they would have already known what He meant. He wasn't purposely trying to hide anything from them. In fact, He gave them plenty of hints. Like this explanation to the Pharisees in Matthew 12:40: "For as Jonah was three days and three nights in the belly of a huge fish, so the Son of Man will be three days and three nights in the heart of the earth."

Nevertheless, they still didn't get it. Sure, they knew the story of Jonah. They heard about his three days in a fish. Now, Jesus told them that He too would be somewhere for three days? Why wouldn't He just give a straight answer?

It must have been frustrating to them. Why did Jesus always like to speak in puzzles? The disciples wondered this as well. As usual, Jesus had a reason: "This is why I speak to them in parables: 'Though seeing, they do not see; though hearing, they do not hear or understand'" (Matthew 13:13). He then quotes Isaiah 6:9, 10, which talks about a people who refuse to see or hear. In other words, Jesus spoke in parables because certain people would not listen anyway. Those who were seeking to know the truth would continue to search. They would search the scriptures. They would remain sitting at Jesus' feet listening for an explanation. Those who did not want to know would not care to search and would be left confused and in the dark.

I'm sure that when Jesus spoke of the sign of Jonah even His disciples had no clue what He meant, otherwise they would not have been surprised at His death. It wouldn't be until after the resurrection that this statement would begin to make sense. This sign of Jonah was Jesus' death and resurrection—the greatest sign given to man regarding Jesus' divinity, love, and authority. Yet not all would recognize this truth. As Paul said: "Jews demand signs and Greeks look for wisdom, but we preach Christ crucified; a stumbling block to Jews and foolishness to Gentiles, but to those whom God has called, both Jews and Greeks, Christ the power of God and the wisdom of God" (1 Corinthians 1:22–24).

The cross is confusing to those only seeking to find miracles or trying to reduce it to simple logic. Their "sight" blinds them. But to the "blind"—those desperately seeking God—the cross is the greatest demonstration of God's power and wisdom. Why? Because at the cross He conquered sin, death, and the grave! For every person searching for God, this sign of love reveals Jesus as our Savior. Of course, if you are not searching—if you are only concerned about yourself—you may think nothing of His death. This is the reason why Jesus, in the parable of the Rich Man and Lazarus, states, "If they do not listen to Moses and the Prophets, they will not be convinced even if someone rises from the dead" (Luke 16:31).

Pharisees may read their scriptures, but it is not to find God. They may excel in their theological studies, but it isn't so they can hear guidance from God's Spirit. Unfortunately, all of their study still leaves them ignorant about God and His love, and as a result they cannot even recognize the greatest sign of all. It is amazing how such a learned group can be so in the dark. If Jesus' death and resurrection couldn't convince them, how could any other miracle? No, Pharisees don't need a sign, they need to be blinded—so Jesus could give them true sight!

The signs and miracles were always meant for those who were seeking. Many came to believe in Jesus because of the signs He gave. Furthermore, these and other signs were to accompany all of those who believe in Him (Mark 16:17, 19). As we've already read, Jesus said, "I tell you the truth, anyone who has faith in me will do what I have been doing. He will do even greater things than these, because I am going to the Father" (John 14:12). We must be careful not to assume that signs and miracles themselves are bad. Actually, Jesus said that they *should* be a part of the lives of His followers.

This is not to say, though, that signs in and of themselves are verification of divine authority. Jesus warned that not all signs performed are from God: "For false christs and false prophets will appear and perform signs and miracles to deceive the elect—if that were possible" (Mark 13:22). It is important to note that Jesus said this in His discussion on the signs of the last days. Even more alarming is that the purpose of *these* signs is an attempt to deceive the elect. We need to be more alert now than ever! Concerning the last days, Paul also warns, "The coming of the lawless one will be in accordance with the work of Satan displayed in all kinds of counterfeit miracles, signs and wonders" (2 Thessalonians 2:9). So, not only will signs accompany the believers in the last days but there will also be counterfeit signs accompanying false christs and false prophets.

This is another reason why Jesus refused to perform a sign as proof: signs and miracles can be counterfeited. Thus, we cannot rely on a miracle to verify divine acceptance. I can assure you that if you become too confident in your own sight—your own ability to recognize the true things of God—you will walk right into the deception. Your "sight" is worthless for spiritual things. Be honest with yourself—are you *absolutely* sure you can tell the difference between a true and a counterfeit miracle? Why take the chance on your own perception? Since signs and miracles will be performed both by good and bad in these last days, you must learn to rely less on yourself and more on Christ.

Some of you might fight this idea because you want to believe you can see more than you really can. When you can see, you are independent; when you are blind, you are dependent. A Pharisee does not want to be dependent on anyone, yet is still spiritually blind. We are not able to truly see unless we are given sight, and it is Jesus' disciples who are given this sight (Matthew 13:11).

So God calls us to fully depend on Him. The Bible is all about dependence. This is why the Bible urges us to seek. We are to seek God's righteousness and His kingdom (Matthew 6:33), seek Him and His presence continually (1 Chronicles 16:11; Psalm 105:4), and seek His face (2 Chronicles 7:14; Psalm 27:8). We are counseled to set our mind and heart to seek God (1 Chronicles 22:19), and to seek Him with all of our heart and soul (Psalm 119:2).

And we will not search in vain. God encourages us with this beautiful promise: "You will seek me and find me when you seek me with all your heart" (Jeremiah 29:13, see also Deuteronomy 4:29 and 2 Chronicles 15:4). God is not trying to trick you. He wants you to find Him. As a matter of fact, He promises that you *will* find Him. But you have to want it. You need to seek Him with everything you are. It is a desperate search: "You God, are my God, earnestly I seek you; I thirst for you, my whole being longs for you, in a dry and parched land where there is no water" (Psalm 63:1). It is in this desperation that you are promised to find Him.

You could always try to sharpen your spiritual observation skills and try to out-do the Pharisees. Maybe you can study more. Perhaps you could attend, or watch, more lectures and sermons. You might learn from the greatest teachers and even get a really thick church-approved, leather-bound Study Bible. Who knows, you might get a few things right every now and then, but without spiritual sight from God, in the long run you will miss the greatest moment of your life: Jesus, right in front of you.

Chapter Nine

"To the Jews who had believed Him, Jesus said, 'If you hold to my teaching, you are really my disciples. Then you will know the truth and the truth will set you free.'"

– JOHN 8:31, 32

Most of the Truth and Nothing More

Imagine sitting in a courtroom. The air is stuffy and tense. All is silent, save for a lone cough in the back of the room. A high profile trial is in progress. The stakes are life and death; there can be no errors on either side. The prosecution and the defense have already presented their opening arguments and the key witnesses are being brought in to testify. The first witness takes the stand and the court officer approaches with a Bible in hand. "Place your right hand on the Bible," He says. The witness complies. The officer continues, "Do you swear to tell most of the truth and nothing more?" Wait! *What?*

We all know that this scenario is not likely to happen. I do not believe there is any legitimate courtroom where this attitude would be acceptable. In cases where people need to make the best judgment *all of the truth* is important, not just most of the truth.

Yet, it seems that today, in Christianity, this approach is becoming less desired. To many people these days, most of the truth is more than enough.

This thinking was already on the rise in the days of Jesus. It most likely caused Jesus to make this seemingly, odd statement to His disciples: "Be on guard against the yeast of the Pharisees and Sadducees" (Matthew 16:5). Beware of yeast?

Immediately, the disciples think Jesus is referring to their weak memories: they forgot to bring bread. Sadly, the disciples must have already forgotten their most recent experience when Jesus fed five thousand (even more than that since they only counted the men!) with only some loaves of bread and a few fish. No, Jesus wasn't reprimanding them for forgetting bread. Nor was He warning them against buying some kind of butter-crusted, twelve-grain, Pharisee-brand bread. It was something much more important: Jesus was warning them against the teachings of the Pharisees and the Sadducees (Matthew 5:12), which He also calls hypocrisy (Luke 12:1).

We've already learned about one side of this. We know Jesus reprimanded them for teaching one thing and then doing another. But there was another dangerous aspect of their teachings that Jesus was warning about: it often included only *most* of the truth.

This became even more evident as Jesus taught. Many times Jesus began a teaching moment by saying, "You've heard it said, but I tell you." Jesus had to frequently re-educate the people on the full truth. "You've heard it said," pointed directly to the popular teachings of the leadership. "But I tell you," revealed that those teachings were incomplete. Every time Jesus taught, He seemed to turn one of their teachings on its head, or He illustrated just how lacking their education was.

One might imagine that Jesus filling in the blanks would be a good thing. You'd think that people professing to follow God would want to know the full truth. Unfortunately the Pharisees did not. The more Jesus taught, the more holes appeared in their own teachings and, well, you could say they didn't care for that.

But, Jesus knew the danger in their acceptance of incomplete truths. He called them out on it during His "woes" in Matthew 23. He said they could put on a good show by building tombs for prophets and decorating graves for them. And at first glance, it would appear as though they had a deep respect for those who came with counsel from God. Yet, He warns, the reality was that they would do the same as their fathers did: kill those who come to teach them more (Matthew 23:29–34).

Israel had a bad reputation for dealing with God's messengers in this way. Whenever God saw His people move away from Him and His counsel, He would send them a prophet to bring them back. God would reveal more light through the prophet to guide those willing to follow. However, those who had made the choice to stop walking—to stop advancing in the truth of God—resisted such guidance. Then, they would take out their displeasure on the messengers. Sadly, one such messenger was even murdered right in the courtyard of the sanctuary (Matthew 23:35)!

Not all prophets were killed, though. Their resistance usually started out a bit more subtle. The way the people treated Jeremiah is one example. Some of them got together and decided to make plans against Him. Their perspective was that the teachings they currently possessed were enough and were not going anywhere, so why would they need to listen to or learn anything more from Jeremiah? Their resolution: "Let us attack him with our tongues and pay no attention to anything he says" (Jeremiah 18:18). They may not have decided to kill him, but they wanted to destroy any influence he might have by verbal attacks and "officially" ignored him (the worst kind of ignoring).

While this reaction may not seem that harsh—probably because we see it so often today—it is the beginning of a dangerous pattern. This reaction is often evidence that one has stopped following God. Think about it: if God sends someone to you to guide you closer to Him, but you refuse to listen, what does that say about your feelings toward God? You cannot say that you are a follower of God if you do not care to listen to His guidance (1 John 1:6).

Most often, the reason we stop following God is because we have found someone else to follow. Sadly, we may not even realize we have stopped following. The Pharisees would have been the last to admit that they weren't following God, but their own words condemned them: "We are disciples of Moses!" they arrogantly declared (John 9:28). Moses had given them all they needed to know. Since Moses stopped teaching (which is a common side-effect of being dead), they stopped learning (a common side-effect of being spiritually dead). In their ignorant arrogance, they made the messenger, Moses, into their god rather than acknowledging the One True God—the Source of the message.

Little did they know, they weren't disciples of Moses after all. No, it was much worse. Jesus explained to them, and to us, that if they were truly following God—if God was their Father—they would accept and follow Him too. But they weren't following Him. So why was it difficult for them to accept Jesus and His teachings? Because: "You belong to your father, the devil, and you want to carry out your father's desire" (John 8:44). Wow! By not following Jesus, they weren't following Moses; they were actually following the devil! Jesus continued, "He was a murderer from the beginning, not holding to the truth, for there is no truth in him . . . he is a liar and the father of lies" (John 8:44). Lies and partial truths are the devil's territory, not God's. The devil is the one who creates comfort in partial truths. He's the one who teaches contentment in stopping halfway in truth. Anyone who stops walking forward in the light of God has become satisfied with resting in the darkness of the adversary. What a sobering thought!

It may be hard to imagine how followers of God would find themselves following the enemy instead. It is not always a conscious decision. Like sheep, sometimes we might discover ourselves in darkness because we have strayed away (Isaiah 53:6), or have been led astray by false shepherds (Jeremiah 50:6). Paul warns that such sheep-stealing deception will continue and even come from those inside our own churches (Acts 20:30). Understand that regardless of the location from which the message is being delivered—whether from your favorite Christian preacher, author, or other religious media source—anyone teaching diluted truth is *never* sent from God. Consider what Paul says in 1 Timothy 6:

> If anyone teaches false doctrines and does not agree to the sound instruction of our Lord Jesus Christ and to godly teaching, he is conceited and understands nothing. He has an unhealthy interest in controversies and quarrels about words that result in envy, strife, malicious talk, evil suspicions and constant friction between men of corrupt mind, who have been robbed of the truth and who think that godliness is a means to financial gain. (Verses 3–5)

He says that such teachers are out for their own benefit. They are willing to compromise the gospel to gain followers. Sadly, these false teachers will distort truth to steal your discipleship to themselves.

But there is good news! If you have found yourself in this situation—feeling more distant from God than you remember or just feeling lost in your Christian journey, led away by popular teachings—then you are among the very people Jesus came to seek and to save (Luke 19:10)! You don't have to remain lost, but you will have to accept the fact that you are. Then, once you admit that you have lost your way, you can be led back to the light of truth by returning to Jesus, the True Shepherd.

However, sometimes we leave God because we don't really want to know more. Maybe we think His rules are too strict or too hard to understand. Maybe we don't like all the changes. Maybe we want to stay in our comfort zone. Either way, we are tired of following Him. In this case, we are *choosing* to leave. Paul told Timothy this would occur:

> For the time will come when men will not put up with sound doctrine. Instead, to suit their own desires, they will gather around them a great number of teachers to

say what their itching ears want to hear. They will turn their ears away from the truth and turn aside to myths. (2 Timothy 4:3, 4)

This creates a vicious circle: they become tired of the whole truth so they surround themselves with those who teach what they *want* to hear—partial truths—which, in turn, makes them less likely to want to hear the full truth afterwards. This "itchy-ear" syndrome is evident in the reactions of the Pharisees. What about you? Have your ears become itchy?

If you have ventured this direction, you would recognize it by your desire to only hear, or study, subjects that are pleasing to you or fit your current lifestyle. You'd find yourself resisting anything that might challenge or change your current views. Perhaps, you only want to hear warm, fuzzy sermons. You love the studies on love and mercy, but you become uncomfortable, irritated even, when obedience or rules are brought up. Or maybe you prefer the tough-love studies that emphasize the law and strict adherence to it. You enjoy hearing a sermon presenting a new rule, or rebuking the non-observance of an old one, but get annoyed and irate if "free grace" or "by faith" is mentioned. Of course, you might just want to continue in the teachings you've always heard. You don't like change and even get angry if someone suggests that one of your beloved teachings is incomplete, or worse yet, wrong! It really doesn't matter which type best describes you, since you will turn the channel, change churches, or stop attending a Bible study simply because you do not really want to hear what the Scriptures actually teach— you are satisfied with the amount of truth you already have.

Sadly, this mindset is much more difficult to overcome. And, those who stubbornly remain in this group will "perish because they refused to love the truth and so be saved" (2 Thessalonians 2:10). This is because a person who does not desire the truth, will fall for every deception and lie.

Yet, even in this seemingly impossible situation, there is hope! God still calls His people to return to Him—to turn away from the darkness and walk in His light. He wants all to come a full knowledge of His truth (1 Timothy 2:4). So He sends the Holy Spirit to draw us back to Himself. Jesus said the Holy Spirit would "guide us into all truth" (John 16:13). God may call you back through a sermon, or through a book, or through a conversation with someone led by His Spirit.

In fact, God sent Paul out with the ministry "to open their eyes and turn them from darkness to light, and from the power of Satan to God, so that they may receive forgiveness of sins and a place among those who are sanctified by faith in me" (Acts 26:18). God called Paul, and still calls many like him today, to reach out to people in darkness. What if God sent someone into *your* life to "open" your eyes and lead you out of the darkness? What would your reaction be? I urge you, do not reject God's rescue attempts like the Pharisees did!

You see, the solution to this problem is to return to the feet of Jesus as a student. If you're not at His feet now, come back! Jesus promises that if you will hold to *His* teachings, "then you will know the truth" (John 8:32). Pharisees refuse to be students; they've become comfortable in partial truths. But when you are following God, partial truth is never enough; you'll always want the *full* truth. Then, like David, this will be your prayer: "Guide me in your truth and teach me, for you are God my savior, and my hope is in you all day long" (Psalm 25:5).

Chapter Ten

"Anyone who runs ahead and does not continue in the teachings of Christ does not have God; whoever continues in the teaching has both the Father and the Son."

— 2 JOHN 9

More Perfecter Than Thou

I was one of those kids who had to walk to school. And, unlike the stories my dad would tell, I really did have to walk uphill both ways! (Technically, it was partially uphill both ways since there was a large hill in between our house and the school.) Needless to say, the walk to and from school wasn't the highlight of my day. I often found myself bored. So I would pass the time by picking up a stick and peeling the bark off of it while I walked. Although this was a solution to my boredom dilemma, it frequently irritated my walking partner (my older sister). Part of the problem was that since I would concentrate too much on my stick, or whatever other distraction I could find, I would fall pretty far behind. Several times during our journey, she would turn around to see how far I had fallen back. Finally, exasperated, she would put her hands on her hips and yell (sometimes I was really far back), "Bill, hurry up!"

Most of the time, I would just pick up the pace and catch up—only to fall behind again. I wasn't long before I became tired of her constant shouting at me. So, one day, when she stood far ahead, hands-on-hips, yelling for me to speed up, a solution popped into my mind. I ran as fast as I could, passed her, and when I had gained some distance ahead of her, I stopped, put my hands on my hips and yelled for *her* to "hurry up!" Just thinking of the look on her face still makes me giggle.

I'll admit, it was very childish (of course, I *was* still a child), but at the time it felt good. She wasn't the only one who could be fast, or yell for that matter. I wanted to prove that I could be as good as her—better even! So I beat her at her own game. Only she wasn't playing.

In the last chapter, we discovered how the teachings of the Pharisees and Sadducees were regularly found wanting; they often only desired most of the truth because they stopped following God. Yet there was another, similarly problematic, issue with their teachings: they often added rules God never required. In other words, they also ran ahead.

Now, don't get me wrong—rules not found in the Bible are not automatically evil. Sometimes it is necessary to create rules for a specific group to govern or protect them—but it is another thing to slide man's rules up to divine status. You see, the Pharisees had established many standards to help protect the people of Israel. But, eventually, these man-made rules became just as important, if not more important, than those rules that were God-breathed.

A perfect illustration of this is the infamous hand-washing incident in Mark 7. Actually, it was more of a failure to wash hands incident. Mark records that a group of Pharisees, along with a few of the scribes, came to see Jesus and happened to catch the disciples dirty handed. They noticed that the disciples ate *without washing their hands.* (I'm not even allowed to do that!) Needless to say, they immediately questioned Jesus on this: "Why don't your disciples live according to the traditions of the elders instead of eating their food with defiled hands?" (Mark 7:5).

You may be wondering why this was so important to them. It wasn't because they were afraid that their mothers would catch them with filthy hands and be disappointed. Nor were they simply being health conscious. Actually, this practice was a long-standing tradition among the elders of Israel (the leadership). According to this passage, the elders would not eat unless they had washed their hands (verses 3 and 4 list other such traditions). Thus, they were surprised that Jesus, a man who many people claimed was godly, would neglect teaching His disciples such an important tradition. All of the most respected leaders and teachers held to these traditions! Why not Jesus and His disciples?

Now, I'm going to guess that this specific tradition itself was not what was important here, because they would have probably tried to charge Him on breaking any one of their traditions. What really frustrated this group was how Jesus paid no attention to *their* cherished rules and traditions! I will also suggest that if it were something God truly desired, Jesus would have also been doing it. But He wasn't (see Luke 11:38).

Again, this doesn't mean that traditions are necessarily against God. Traditions can be good. Washing your hands before a meal can keep you from getting sick. However, the Pharisees' hand washing tradition had been taken one step further. According to them, by not following this tradition—washing your hands before you eat—your hands would become "unclean." This isn't referring to being simply dirty; it means "common," as in, not able to enter the Temple to offer a sacrifice to God. It was basically the same penalty as someone who contracted leprosy. In other words, if you didn't wash your hands before you ate, you would not be able to present yourself before God.

Did God really say that? Is there a passage in Scripture where God called someone unclean because they did not wash their hands? (Maybe it's in the book of Hezekiah*.) Actually, no, God has never said anything like that. Yet, the Pharisees had taken this tradition—one that most likely started with good intention—and placed it above God's Word. On top of that, they were even trying to require God Himself to follow it! As if He didn't already know, and uphold, all the rules.

I saw this mindset demonstrated once. A gentleman had come to talk with me and the conversation somehow got around to diet. He was very passionate as he talked about his thoughts on diet and ended with a statement that took me off guard. He said, "A person must be a vegetarian to be saved." To make sure I didn't misunderstand him, he said bluntly that eating meat is a sin. Now, I will not deny there are health benefits in a vegetarian lifestyle, but nowhere in Scripture does it say that eating meat is a sin. So, in an attempt to prompt further discussion and reconsideration, I brought up the Achilles heel of his statement: what about Jesus? He ate meat and yet the Bible says He didn't sin. The man looked at me very seriously and said, "He didn't have the full truth like we do, otherwise He would have been vegetarian too."

I could not believe my ears. *We* have more truth than Jesus? He was basically saying that Jesus didn't know any better! It seemed to me that this man would have been one to stand in line behind the Pharisees waiting to educate Jesus in the ways of proper Christian tradition and lifestyle. Yet another rule had been elevated to divine status without Divine permission—another person running ahead of God. Many, unfortunately, leave such rules unquestioned and blindly start to follow the tradition.

Jesus, however, does no such thing. We do not read of Him apologizing and running off to the nearest sink to wash up. It is not written that Jesus pulls a bottle of hand-sanitizer out of His robe, blesses it, and distributes it among His disciples. Instead, He points out the reality of *their* beloved traditions:

> Isaiah was right when he prophesied about you hypocrites; as it is written: "These people honor me with their lips, but their hearts are far from me. They worship me in vain, their teachings are but rules taught by men." You have let go of the commands of God and are holding on to the traditions of men. (Mark 7:6–8)

I wonder what their reaction to this statement must have been. My guess is that it would have stirred them up, only because I can imagine how people today would respond. We are not told that the Pharisees lowered their heads in humility and accepted the correction of Jesus. If anything, they probably held their heads a little higher and fumed at the statements of, in their opinion, such an uneducated person. He thought He was so perfect! Well, they were . . . more perfecter!

Of course, Jesus wasn't finished. He gives examples of how they set aside God's commands in order to keep their own teachings. With this mindset, people often bypass God's teachings in favor of their own. In fact, He states, "you nullify the word of God by your own tradition that you have handed down. And you do many things like that" (Mark 7:13). And they did. For example, they refused to accept Him because He broke the Sabbath—well, He broke *their* traditions regarding the Sabbath at least (John 9:16). Unfortunately, this attitude stuck with some of them even after choosing to follow Christ (Acts 15:1–21). It seems that some habits are hard to break.

You may wonder how a person can come to such an attitude. It can be seen in Jesus' statement that, once again, selfishness and pride are involved. Paul confirms this in Romans 16:17, 18. He says that people who create obstacles that are contrary to the teachings of Christ are out for personal gain. They are serving their own appetites and not serving Jesus. In 1 Timothy 6:3–5, Paul goes even further and states that those who teach a different doctrine than Christ taught (going beyond His teachings) are conceited and understand nothing. Therefore, adding to God's teachings is mainly about pride and personal gain.

Sadly, the Bible prophesies that such false teachers and false teachings would continue down through the last days. We are told in 1 Timothy 4:1–8 that some will abandon following God and will follow after godless myths. It will partially be the result of teachings by hypocritical, self-serving liars. Yet, another reason is because people will simply not want to hear sound truth and will seek out teachers to teach what they want to hear (2 Timothy 4:3, 4). Either way, the outcome is the same: they will no longer be walking with Christ.

You see, if you are not walking with Christ and following Him, you will either stop short of full truth (see previous chapter), or you will run ahead and find yourself among teachings and traditions Jesus never spoke of.

Someone might argue that it would be better to run ahead than it would be to stop all together. But neither of these options is healthy. Both are still not *with* Christ. John says, "Anyone who runs ahead and does not continue in the teaching of Christ does not have God; whoever continues in the teaching has both the Father and the Son" (2 John 9). You may think you are improving yourself, but if you run ahead, you are still leaving God's side!

Unfortunately, we have fallen prey to the deception that when we add our own rules and traditions we add value to our religious experience. We sometimes think that what God gave us is cake, but what we add is icing on the cake. However, this couldn't be further from the truth. The journey with Christ is best when you are right beside Him, walking with Him, not ahead of Him or behind. In fact, if you're not beside Him, you're not really walking with Him!

Hebrews 11 is filled with stories of people who had incredible journeys with God. They are not recorded there because of some unique teaching they added, but because of their willingness to depend wholly on what God said. Following God was enough. Paul thought so too:

So then, just as you received Christ Jesus as Lord, continue to live your lives in him, rooted and built up in him, strengthened in the faith as you were taught, and overflowing with thankfulness. See to it that no one takes you captive through hollow and deceptive philosophy, which depends on human tradition and the elemental spiritual forces of this world rather than on Christ. (Colossians 2:6–8)

You started with Christ; finish with Christ. Living *in* Christ requires you to be quite close to Him. Being rooted and built up in Him requires that you be attached to Him. But Paul warns us that there are teachers who will want to make us captives of a teaching or tradition that has us depending on the wisdom of this world or human tradition rather than God. Don't let them! Why?

> Since you died with Christ to the elemental spiritual forces of this world, why, as though you still belonged to the world, do you submit to its rules: "Do not handle! Do not taste! Do not touch!"? These rules, which have to do with things that are all destined to perish with use, are based on merely human commands and teachings. Such regulations indeed have an appearance of wisdom, with their self-imposed worship, their false humility and their harsh treatment of the body, but they lack any value in restraining sensual indulgence [lit. *indulgences of the flesh*—it is not necessarily sensual]. (Colossians 2:20–23, notes mine)

According to Paul, man-made teachings may look good and seem wise, but they aren't worth anything in overcoming any of our sinful desires. Therefore, following human traditions cannot add any extra value or holiness to your walk with Christ. They are empty and will fade away like a fad.

Besides, think about it: God's counsel for us in Scripture already covers everything we need for salvation. What more *could* we add? Is there some technique God failed to remember? Did God leave out a vital tradition that would make us the "most holiest" possible? Can we teach God anything about righteous living? Of course not!

Instead, God's Word urges us to stick with what Christ taught. Jesus said, "If you hold to my teaching, you are really my disciples" (John 8:31). Of course, He wants you to hold on to His teachings because they are capable of transforming you. They are the Word of God that will sanctify you (John 17:17). *His* teachings are what you are to pass on to new disciples (Matthew 28:20).

Moreover, He told us that the promised Holy Spirit would come to "teach you all things and will remind you of everything I have said to you" (John 14:26). Every disciple who received the Holy Spirit would be led to, or reminded of, His teachings and, as His disciple, would hold on to them. And this desire to hold on to His teachings will also be an identifying factor of His followers until He comes (Revelation 12:17).

Of course, how can one tell if something is a teaching of Jesus? Notice what Jesus says: "My teaching is not my own. It comes from the one who sent me. Anyone who chooses to do the will of God will find out whether my teaching comes from God or whether I speak on my own" (John 7:16, 17).

Jesus is not going to contradict what the Father has already spoken and tells us that if we truly desire to follow God's will, we will be able to know when a teaching is from God. This is why we are told in Scripture to test things that claim to be of God and hold on to only that which is true (see 1 Thessalonians 5:20, 21 and 1 John 4:1). Therefore, you should test any, and every, teaching or tradition that is claiming to be of God against what He has already said in His Word. Isaiah 8:20 says that "if anyone does not speak according to this word, they have no light of dawn." In other words, if the Scriptures do not already support the teaching, it is not truth (light) and it is not from God. Such teachings, no matter how cherished, have no value in our spiritual walk and should be put in their proper place (some should probably be thrown out completely).

It is not wrong or offensive to question a teaching or tradition, because the truth can stand up to scriptural scrutiny. In fact, a group from the city of Berea was called more noble because "they received the message with great eagerness and examined the Scriptures every day to see if what Paul said was true" (Acts 17:11). They even tested what Paul was preaching!

So test! Test everything! Test what is spoken this weekend from the pulpit. Test what you hear from a Christian radio station. Test what is written in this book. Do not take anything as truth until you have examined it for yourself in Scripture. See what God says and hold on to that. For God alone is the source of truth.

The Pharisees were only focused on themselves and their teachings and traditions revealed this. If you, too, are only focused on yourself or the things of this world, you will miss out on the truth of God and follow after myths created by man. But if you seek to follow Christ and do His will, you *will* be led to the Truth of His teachings! Whenever you do find His truth—whether it was a long time ago, or just recently—don't let it go! Hold tight!

---

*In case you are trying to find the book of Hezekiah, I need to admit that there is no such book. Hezekiah was a king of Israel, but he did not write a book (even though it does sound like a book that could be in the Bible!). Any time something is claimed to be in scripture when it is not, I tend to quote from this "book."

Chapter Eleven

"I am the resurrection and the life.
He who believes in me will live, even though he dies."

— JOHN 11:25

They're So Sad, You See

Rumors of the Pharisee's continued humiliation by Jesus spread like wild fire. Every time they set up a trap, He seemed to see right through it. Their most recent attempt had been trying to trick Him by questioning their duty to pay taxes. Yet, so far, all of their traps were unsuccessful. Immediately, the Sadducees wanted another chance (tag-team trappings?).

You may be wondering, why bring up the Sadducees in a book about the Pharisees? Remember, Jesus did warn the disciples about their teachings along with the Pharisees' (Matthew 16:5). They were a group not that different from the Pharisees, yet they hardly ever saw eye-to-eye with them on anything; they often fought over their countless doctrinal differences (see Acts 23:6–8). Well, they didn't agree about anything except for their feelings towards Jesus, I guess. Jesus' presence seemed to draw the two groups together. They had already worked side-by-side on other occasions, like when they wanted to test Him by asking for a sign from heaven (see Matthew 16:1–4). Maybe this was one of those "an enemy of my enemy is a friend" situations. Regardless, the Sadducees joined in on the Pharisees' efforts to try to trap Jesus and begin the downfall of His reputation.

They probably thought this next one up back in a special, secret meeting. They wanted to hit Him with a question that would really cause Him to stumble. He claimed to be from God. They'd see about that! When they finally reached Jesus, they asked their question (the full story can be found in Matthew 22:23–33, Mark 12:18–24, and Luke 20:27–38):

> Teacher, Moses told us that if a man dies without having children, his brother must marry the widow and raise up offspring for him. Now there were seven brothers among us. The first one married and died, and since he had no children, he left his wife to his brother. The same thing happened to the second and third brother, right on down to the seventh. Finally, the woman died. Now then, at the resurrection, whose wife will she be of the seven, since all of them were married to her? (Matthew 22:24–28)

Glancing at each other, they smiled knowingly: there was no way He could answer this! At least not in a manner that would be acceptable *and* in keeping with the Law.

You need to understand that this wasn't really a question on marriage—or marriage in heaven, for that matter—this question was about the resurrection. You see, they had passionate opinions concerning this issue. It was one of their fundamental beliefs. Their understanding of the resurrection separated them from most of the other groups in Israel—it's what placed them above all others (at least in their eyes). So then, what *were* their thoughts concerning the resurrection? They didn't believe there would even be a resurrection (see verse 23).

Let me give you a little history.* The Sadducees, much like the Pharisees, have somewhat unclear beginnings. Some suggest they were a group that came from a man named Zadok, who lived long before the time of Jesus, although there is little evidence to support these legends. What is definite is that the group dated back to the time of the Maccabean wars—again, similar to the Pharisees.

Still, there were several things that separated this group from the rest. It was composed of the nobility, powerful, and wealthy. They were more interested in political issues since many controlled those areas already; many highly influential people were part of the Sadducees, including the High Priest. As a result, the Sadducees became a more exclusive group than even the Pharisees (who were actually considered the group for the common people).

In addition, the Sadducees rejected the oral law, or tradition of the elders, that the Pharisees upheld. Instead, they saw the Torah (the first five books of Moses) as the sole source of their authority. Because of this, any belief or doctrine that was not defined in the first five books of the Bible was thrown out. For instance, they did not share the hope of the Messiah like the rest of Israel. So, instead of entrusting their hope into God's hands, they took the destiny of the nation into their own hands, using their power and influence against any opposing nation. They also refused to accept the Babylonian teaching of the immortality of the soul, which had crept into Israel's theology. Yet, because of this, they also rejected *any* idea of an afterlife—there would be no rewards or penalties after death . . . ever. It is from this position that their rejection of the resurrection takes root. Acts 23:8 tells us that in addition to rejecting the resurrection, they also rejected angels and the idea of spirits (including the Holy Spirit). Since the Torah doesn't discuss these issues, they rejected them. So, Jesus couldn't support the resurrection since there was *clearly* no mention of it in the Torah.

Honestly, the more I learned about the Sadducees' beliefs, the more I felt sorry for them. Here is a group that had no hope of the Messiah, or the resurrection, and rejected the concept of miracles, angels, and spirits (even the Holy Spirit!). All of their hope was in their own power and wealth; not one bit of hope was placed on God. How sad they must have been! What kind of life is it without the hope of the resurrection? Or greater still, what kind of life is it without the hope of the Messiah? Remember, these are professed followers of God, yet without a Messiah.

Ironically, this sad group was having a conversation with *the* Messiah—the One who *is* the Resurrection and the Life! And, of all questions, they ask *Him* about the resurrection.

But it wasn't even really about the resurrection. They really didn't care about the possible answer—which brother the woman might be married to—because, in their minds, there wouldn't be a resurrection in the first place. No, this was purely about trapping Jesus. Okay, it may have been a little bit about plugging their own doctrines as well. Because, let's face it, if Jesus couldn't provide a satisfactory answer, the Sadducees would have the opportunity to drive home what they had been preaching for years. And if His answer supported their teachings, they would easily benefit from His unbelievable popularity. Either way, *they* would gain more power and influence. But it didn't work out that way.

Jesus directly confronted their rejection of the resurrection. "You are wrong," He says. I can assure you that was not the response they were expecting. He boldly claimed that this pillar of their belief system was false. Their question was pointless because their whole approach to the issue was wrong—because they did not "know the Scriptures or the power of God" (Matthew 22:29). Any smug looks on their faces would have fallen at these words. They prided them-selves on their knowledge of the Torah and their strict adherence to it. Yet, Jesus had the audacity to suggest that they didn't even have the basic information on these things.

Jesus then presented the truth concerning the first facet of their question: *at the resurrection* marriage will not be an issue because we will be like the angels. Luke's account adds, "for they cannot die anymore . . . and are sons of God, being sons of the resurrection" (Luke 20:36). [On a side note, some have suggested that this means we will be asexual, being neither male nor female.

Yet, nowhere in Scripture does it mention any kind of sexuality of the angels—asexual or otherwise—so we would be adding this idea to it. Plus, Luke's account helps clarify Jesus' referral to the angels: we cannot die anymore.]

Also, notice that Jesus did not say, "in heaven," but rather, "at the resurrection." On that great day, when Jesus comes in the clouds and the resurrection takes place, I doubt the first thing on anyone's mind will be, "who am I married to?" There won't be wedding ceremonies or feasts occurring in the air on the way to meet Jesus in the clouds. Our focus will be on Jesus! Besides, the laws Moses gave for marriage were necessary in those times, but were not what God originally planned for mankind. Thus, the Sadducees were attempting to limit God's power with laws that governed man, and then use those man-made "limitations" to disprove the resurrection. Jesus' answer reveals more about the resurrection than it does about marriage. He is assuring them, and the crowd around, that there will *definitely* be a resurrection!

That was the heart of the issue: doubt about the resurrection. So Jesus continued with the question: "have you not read?" Of course they had read. They thoroughly studied their scriptures (it must have been easy too, with only five books to learn); they knew which passages Jesus was referring to. In His response, Jesus quoted from the only part of scripture they would have accepted and *still proved the resurrection!* (When will we ever learn? We cannot trap Jesus!) Their scriptures said, and the Israelites proudly claimed, that God is the God of Abraham, Isaac, and Jacob (their nation's founding forefathers). In fact, this is always stated in present tense: God *is* their God, not *was* their God. If the Sadducees' concept of resurrection was correct—that this life is all we have and after death there is nothing—how could God be Abraham's God *in the present tense*? Since God is God of the living and not the dead, there would have to be a resurrection, and a life after life, for Him to be their God.

Their error was that they did not *know* the scripture or the power of God. Instead of striving to learn more about the God of the Scriptures, they had crammed God into their own ideas. In order to do that, they needed to reject evidence of God's power (any power that wasn't already revealed in the first five books). Imagine it from their way of thinking: if God were really *that* powerful, what would be the use for *their* power or authority? What a horrible thought!

This is unfortunately typical: when man designs a god, that god's power and existence is fully dependent on man; because the created is always subject to its creator. If God sometimes seems limited and weak to you, you might want to examine your ideas of God and see if you have attempted to confine Him to a box *you* created. Because, according to Scripture, God is not the one with limitations—we are. As Jesus said, "With man this is impossible, but with God all things are possible" (Matthew 19:26).

As if limiting God wasn't bad enough by itself, by rejecting the true power of God and its evidence in Scriptures, they were also rejecting salvation itself! In their rejection of the resurrection, the Sadducees removed all hope of eternal life. In their rejection of the resurrection they were also rejecting Jesus, "the resurrection and the life" (John 11:25). They didn't understand the power of God because they refused to accept any evidence concerning it. It all seemed like foolishness to them. Spirits and angels? Miracles? The resurrection of *dead* people? It just wasn't logical. What they embraced was the power of humanity. They believed in, and relied on, mankind's ability to get things done on their own.

The cross, then, would seem just as ridiculous to them. What good could come from such a death? In their way of thinking, His death would only further prove their points. First, by dying, Jesus could not have been God, and if He was, He obviously wasn't very powerful—He died! Second, if Jesus were God, why would He allow His ministry and influence to be cut off so abruptly? It would be more foolishness. They would never be able to see it as evidence of the power of God (1 Corinthians 1:18). Similar to the Pharisees, the Sadducees allowed themselves to get in the way of accepting Christ. Their love for position and power, and their narrow focus on the law, led to their missing the freedom of the gospel.

Sadly, there are still Sadducees today. There are still people who refuse to completely rely on Christ due to their love for authority and influence. Their views of God will be narrow—rejecting whole portions of Scripture because it doesn't match their preconceived ideas. A modern Sadducee will still be enticed by high positions, political influence, and self-help teachings. Any notion of salvation through dependence will be rejected. The pure gospel is thrown out. It is seen as cheap, unnecessary, and inadequate. Jesus may be seen as *part* of the solution for sin, but not all of the solution—man has to work out the remainder. Thus, anyone living as a Sadducee will attempt to use position, influence, or authority—man's power and wisdom—to "get things done" for God.

Yet, the Bible tells us not to trust in ourselves. Proverbs 3:5 says, "Trust in the LORD with all your heart and lean not on your own understanding." In Jeremiah, God says: "Cursed is the one who trusts in man, who draws strength from mere flesh and whose heart turns away from the LORD.' . . . But blessed is the man who trusts in the LORD, whose confidence is in him" (Jeremiah 17:5, 7).

This is because our own understanding is flawed; our "wisdom" is limited. We may think something is right, but find it only leads us further away from God (Proverbs 14:12). Therefore, God reveals His power through man so we will choose to rely on Him. Paul stated that his lack of speaking skills and limited understanding of the gospel while visiting the people of Corinth allowed the power of the Holy Spirit to be revealed in Him, so that their faith "may not rest on human wisdom, but on God's power" (1 Corinthians 2:5).

In your "strength" you will create an image of an impotent god, while in your weakness God's true strength is revealed. It is the very theme of the gospel: complete dependence on the power of God for salvation. This is why the gospel is so necessary. We are powerless to save ourselves (see Jeremiah 13:23 and Ephesians 2:8, 9). Not even the good things that we do can earn for us salvation (Isaiah 64:6). This is why Paul says, "For I am not ashamed of the gospel, for it is the power of God that brings salvation to everyone who believes" (Romans 1:16).

Friend, the Bible is clear—on your own, there is no hope. None. Why would you want to go through life with no hope? Still, this is the truth: not one person will receive eternal life due to their position in society, their strong moral efforts, or their padded bank accounts. However, if you will depend on God, it is impossible that you will perish, but you *will* receive eternal life (John 3:16). This is God's promise to you: if you depend on Him, He will save you. He can promise this because He has the power to back it up. Search the Scriptures and you'll see this is true!

The real question is, do you believe in the power of God? The Sadducees didn't. They rejected the power of God and refused to accept the free gift of salvation He offered. Do not make that same mistake! May you be among those, on the day Jesus returns, who say: "Surely this is our God, we trusted in Him and He saved us. This is the Lord, we trusted in him; let us rejoice and be glad in His salvation" (Isaiah 25:9).

---

* Information on the Sadducees taken from the writings of Josephus, (Antiquities, 13.10.6); and the online Jewish Encyclopedia (www.jewishencyclopedia.com/articles/12989-sadducees). You can learn more about the Sadducees from these and other fine sources.

Chapter Twelve

"Today if you hear His voice, do not harden your hearts."
— PSALM 95:7, 8

Rare Sightings
of the Unforgiven

Could it be? Was it another rare sighting? How could this happen with so much evidence? Yet, sure enough, there they were. Maybe I need to back up a bit and tell you how they were revealed. You see, Jesus was out and about doing His normal daily activities: healing, teaching, freeing captives, and all other sorts of things that brought tremendous joy to all those who followed (well, almost all). Then, someone brought a demon-possessed man to Jesus. The man was blind and mute, but this was no match for the power of God. So Jesus healed him right then and there, in the sight of everyone, and the man could see and talk. What a moment that must have been! It definitely impacted those who witnessed the miracle. Many began to wonder out loud if Jesus could, in fact, be the promised Messiah, the son of David.

As usual, not everyone present was impressed. When the Pharisees heard what the people were saying, they offered their interpretation of the situation. "Don't get all excited," they said. "This imposter only drives out demons by Beelzebub, the prince of demons." Wow. Really? They don't even suggest that the man was not actually healed but just faking it, or that he was never sick in the first place. They jump right to "the Devil did it." Of course, what else could they say? Jesus was against everything they stood for. Everything He did threatened their never-before-questioned influence. Besides, if they really were the model of holiness and perfection in God, and He wasn't a part of them, then their logic concluded that He couldn't be of God.

Jesus knew their thoughts and reveals the foolishness of their explanation: If Satan drives out Satan, his kingdom is divided and cannot stand. "And if I drive them out through Beelzebub," He suggests, "through whom do your people cast out demons?" Their logic doesn't make sense. Yet, what Jesus says next was clearly a warning to those listening:

> And so I tell you, every sin and blasphemy will be forgiven men, but the blasphemy against the Spirit will not be forgiven. Anyone who speaks a word against the Son of Man will be forgiven, but anyone who speaks against the Holy Spirit will not be forgiven, either in this age or in the age to come. (Matthew 12:31, 32)

A sin or sinner not forgiven? How could this be? There is little question that the Bible is filled with characters that were clearly sinners. Consider Abraham: He is known as the father of nations; many nations point back to him as their founding ancestor, but he was lacking in the truth category. Basically, he didn't trust God so he lied to Pharaoh about his wife not being his wife—not just once, but twice! In addition, he took his handmaid to have a child, even after God said to him that *his wife* was going to have the baby. He ran ahead of God and tried to achieve God's promise through his own method. And yet, after Abraham had done all of these things (and probably many more), God still said he was a friend. So, non-trusting, liar-liar-pants-on-fire Abraham had not committed the unpardonable sin.

What about King David? I won't go into detail, but that whole Bathsheba episode was a mess! He was a known murderer and an adulterer (have you ever wondered how we might treat David in our churches today?), and yet God later said that David was a man after His own heart. Even peeping Tom, adulterer, and murderer David did not commit the unpardonable sin.

Then there's Peter. He denied Jesus three times on the night of His crucifixion—complete with complimentary cursing the third time—and yet the ashamed-to-be-a-disciple Peter with a sailor's mouth had not committed the unpardonable sin. He was forgiven and became a great preacher who, on the Day of Pentecost with the power of the Holy Spirit, brought three thousand people to Christ.

Let's not forget about Paul: he stood by and held the coats of the people stoning Stephen. He'd become a well-known persecutor of Christians, and yet God converted him and chose him to be one of the first missionaries to the Gentiles. Thus, even Paul, the infamous oppressor of Christians, had not committed the unpardonable sin.

None of these great sinners had committed the unpardonable sin. Why? Because, as great a sinner we may be, our Savior is greater! This is why we have such promises as 1 John 1:9, which says, "If we confess our sins, He is faithful and just and will forgive us our sins and purify us from all unrighteousness." Or, Hebrews 8:12, "For I will forgive their wickedness and will remember their sins no more."

With this kind of forgiveness, how can there still be a sin that is unpardonable? According to Jesus, blasphemy and speaking against the Holy Spirit will not be forgiven. The definition of the Greek word for blasphemy is "to defame; to harm someone's reputation." Interestingly, this same word is used at Jesus' trial when the soldiers "mocked" Him. This, Jesus says, is unforgivable: speaking against, defaming, or mocking the Holy Spirit.

The Bible gives us three examples of blasphemy. The first one is found in the story we just read: the Pharisees credited Satan for something Jesus says only the Holy Spirit could do (see Matthew 12:22–24). Jesus warned them that this attitude was blasphemy against the Spirit.

The next example, found in another accusation of Jesus by the Pharisees, reveals another facet of blasphemy: "When Jesus saw their faith, he said, 'Friend, your sins are forgiven.' The Pharisees and the teachers of the law began thinking to themselves, 'Who is this fellow who speaks blasphemy? Who can forgive sins but God alone?'" (Luke 5:20, 21). Here they accused Jesus of blasphemy because He had the audacity to forgive sins, something only God can do. They accused Jesus of mocking God by claiming to have the authority to forgive sins Himself (of course, He *did* have the power and authority to forgive sins).

The third example is similar:

> Again the Jews picked up stones to stone him, but Jesus said to them, "I have shown you many great miracles from the Father. For which of these do you stone me?" "We are not stoning you for any of these," replied the Jews, "but for blasphemy, because you, a mere man, claim to be God" (John 10:31–33)

This time, Jesus was accused by the Jews of defaming God because He, a "mere man," claimed to *be* God.

These are the three examples of the biblical understanding of blasphemy. They focus on taking credit away from God by giving credit to someone else or taking the credit ourselves. Therefore, if hurting the reputation of the Holy Spirit is unforgivable, we must be careful not to take credit away from the Holy Spirit for things only He can do.

You may be wondering why this sin is worse. We get a better understanding if we learn more about the Holy Spirit. The Bible says that God's Spirit was present at creation (Genesis 1:2). The Spirit has been among us since creation but, unfortunately, people have not always accepted Him (Genesis 6:3). However, His Spirit was still active among the people of God throughout the Old Testament, and was responsible for inspiring all that was written in God's Word (2 Peter 1:21). We also know that when Jesus was baptized, God's Spirit was there: the Spirit descended upon Jesus like a dove (Matthew 3:16) and filled Him with power. Later, He promised that the Holy Spirit would come upon His disciples and give them the same power to finish the work of the Kingdom (Acts 1:8). Furthermore, the Holy Spirit is promised to everyone who follows Him (Acts 2:38).

What is the reason for this gift? Jesus said that the Holy Spirit would teach us and remind us of everything Jesus taught (John 14:26). He also said that the Holy Spirit would guide us into all truth (John 16:13). Not just part of the truth but all of the truth. God sends us the gift of His Spirit to lead us further in Truth and bring back to our minds the teachings of Jesus. Yet there's more:

> Unless I go away, the Counselor will not come to you; but if I go, I will send him to you. When he comes, he will convict the world of guilt in regard to sin and righteousness and judgment: in regard to sin, because men do not believe in me; in regard to righteousness, because I am going to the Father, where you can see me no longer; and in regard to judgment, because the prince of this world now stands condemned. (John 16:7–11)

Conviction is a major work of the Spirit of God. The Holy Spirit convicts us of our sin. How can we repent of our rebellion if we are not convicted of it? The Spirit helps us see that Jesus is the Way, and that we need Him. We wouldn't recognize our need of Jesus on our own without God's Spirit. The Spirit also convicts us of righteousness. When Jesus ascended into heaven, His visible example of righteousness was gone. But the Holy Spirit convicts us of the way we should go and leads us in the right path. We wouldn't know which way to go without the Spirit. Finally, the Spirit convicts mankind of judgment. The Holy Spirit was also sent to convict us of a coming judgment in which every one of us is going to have to make a decision to either follow God or reject Him. The devil knows his time is short; without the Spirit, we would not recognize the urgency of the situation.

Can you imagine what would happen to those following God if we did not have His Spirit to convict us? If not for the Holy Spirit, none of us would be convicted of anything regarding our spiritual life. We need this conviction because there's a war going on for our souls! The Holy Spirit leads us to the eternal gospel of God, and the Adversary, with all of his rebellious angels, is trying to draw us away from it. God sends His Spirit to us so we can have the guidance and power we need to faithfully follow Him. "Whether you turn to the right or to the left, your ears will hear a voice behind you, saying, 'This is the way; walk in it'" (Isaiah 30:21).

Now consider this in light of Jesus' statement of blasphemy. He is warning us that if we take the credit for the work of the Holy Spirit (conviction, guidance, declaring what is truth, etc.), or give the credit to the enemy (or anyone else for that matter), we are committing a sin that is unforgivable. Why? Because, this harms the character of the Holy Spirit, which, in turn, reduces (or removes) the impact the Spirit can have in our life, and the lives of those around us. Think about it: if I can claim the work of the Spirit as my own, the Spirit must not be as important as God says. If man claims to be the one who convicts, or guides, or reveals what truth is for you—as Pharisees often do—then you might not turn to the Spirit of God for guidance. The consequence is that you would follow man instead of the Spirit. You might wait for your pastor or your church to "convict" you of something instead of listening for God's Spirit. This would not be good.

Another problem that arises is that if the Spirit's work in our lives is credited elsewhere, we would become unaccustomed to recognizing the Spirit. The Pharisees obviously couldn't recognize the Spirit working through Jesus—they were quick to assign the Spirit's work to Satan! This is because they had hardened their hearts to the work of the Spirit in their own lives. They were used to explaining away the works of the Spirit of God whenever those works were contrary to what they desired. And if we get to this point, it becomes very hard to tell when God's Spirit is actually guiding. Eventually, we would resist the Holy Spirit's work in our life simply out of habit. This was an obvious problem with the people in Jesus' day: "You stiff-necked people . . . You are just like your fathers: you always resist the Holy Spirit!" (Acts 7:51). Even though the Holy Spirit still moved among them, they had become resistant, and the Spirit's guidance was lost. This is why Paul tells us: "do not grieve the Holy Spirit of God" (Ephesians 4:30).

Friend, there are still those today who blaspheme the Spirit and will try to convince you to do the same. Do not be like the Pharisees! Do not give someone else credit when a person is healed; that is the power of God's Spirit! Do not take credit when a person is convicted of sin; that is the work of the Spirit!

The Pharisees had become so unaccustomed to recognizing and following God's Spirit, that they easily took credit away from Him. They claimed to be the ones who could guide people to the full truth of God. They believed it was their duty to identify and convict people of their sins. And if it didn't come from them, it must be from the devil. The more often they did this, the less impact the Spirit had in their lives and the lives of those they influenced.

Whenever we attempt to do the work of the Spirit, or refuse to acknowledge His work, we lose our ability to recognize the Spirit working in our lives. And if we no longer recognize the work of the Spirit in our lives, we will reject Him. And when we reject the Holy Spirit, He can't convict of us sin, righteousness, or judgment. When the Spirit is resisted, He can no longer lead us to the Way, the Truth, and the Life. Then this will be the only result we could expect: "If we deliberately keep on sinning after we have received the knowledge of the truth, no sacrifice for sins is left. But only a fearful expectation of judgment and of raging fire that will consume the enemies of God" (Hebrews 10:26, 27).

This is how it is possible that, even in the presence of Christ, you could find yourself unforgiven. By rejecting the real work of

God's Spirit, you could come to a point when you know what God wants you to do (and are able to do it) but refuse to do it. Then, according to the Bible, there only remains a fearful expectation of judgment, since no sacrifice for sins is left. The result of this choice: not forgiven.

Unfortunately, this is not as rare of a sighting as it should be. Too many people today are becoming resistant to the Spirit of God because many are continuing to defame Him. But this does not have to be true about you! Jesus died on the cross to save you from your sins. He offered Himself as a sacrifice for you so that you could receive a full pardon. He didn't come to condemn you, but to change you. He came to pick you up from this rebellion and bring you to a higher place. The result of this choice: forgiven.

Friend, it's God's *desire* to forgive you. He says in Isaiah 1:18, "'Come now, let us reason together,' says the Lord. 'Though your sins are like scarlet, they shall be as white as snow; though they are red as crimson, they shall be like wool.'" And again in 1 John 1:9, "If we confess our sins, he is faithful and just and will forgive us our sins and purify us from all unrighteousness." Yes, the Lord desires to take away your sin, but if you reject the convicting work of the Holy Spirit in your life, and refuse to trust God, how can He take away your sin?

Again, if you resist the Spirit that convicts you of sin, you will not confess your sin. And if you do not confess your sins, how can Jesus forgive them? You need God's Spirit to guide you and convict you. Only the Spirit can convict you of your rebellion against God; no one else can. Only the Spirit can convict you of true righteousness; no one else can. Only the Spirit can convict you that time is short; no one else will. And this Spirit is a gift to *all* who believe.

So, why would you want to mock the One who is working hard for your salvation? Why would you want to tarnish the character, or the influence, of the One who can convict those you love of their need for God? Do not be like the Pharisees and reject the work of the Holy Spirit in your life. Psalms 95:7, 8 says, "Today if you hear His voice, do not harden your hearts."

Chapter Thirteen

"He who has the Son has life; He who does not have the Son of God does not have life. I write these things to you who believe in the name of the Son of God so that you may know that you have eternal life."

– 1 JOHN 5:12, 13

A Battle
with Dandelions

The Kingdom of God is like two men, one wise and one foolish, who moved into homes in an upscale community in which they were required to keep a lush, green lawn— only to find their lawns overrun by dandelions. The foolish man, embarrassed by the sight of such failure in his lawn, immediately ran out with shears and began to cut off the tops of all the flowers. Day after day he battled with those persistent, golden weeds, until he was satisfied that he had conquered every one. Yet, to his dismay, he soon found even more dandelions growing. Some eventually matured and grew white and fluffy. Not to be defeated, the man huffed and puffed and blew each one away, until there were no more snowy puffs in his lawn. Every day the foolish man battled with the dandelions; every day they grew in number and in size. Soon, the foolish man's lawn was nothing but weeds.

The wise man, also embarrassed by the vision of yellow blooms dotting his yard, called on the Master Gardener to come and clean up his lawn. He watched as the Master Gardener sprayed some, pulled some, and seemingly ignored others completely. Although he didn't understand the Master Gardener's methods, he left the care of his lawn completely in the Gardener's skilled hands. After the first day, the wise man saw no noticeable improvement in his predicament. Yet, after a few days and weeks passed, he began to notice fewer weeds in his yard. Not only were there less dandelions, but the whole yard was stronger, healthier, and greener. Soon, through the dedicated work of the Gardener, the wise man's lawn had no dandelions, only a lush, green healthy lawn.

We have already learned that the Pharisees were well-known for their personal attempts at salvation. They strove to keep their lives looking holy—at least to those watching. Yet, Jesus was clear that their attempts were not good enough. His teachings made it clear that there was a different path to true righteousness. So, as many in His day wondered, if our efforts to clean up our lives are ineffective towards salvation, and we stop trying to do it ourselves, how *can* we have the assurance of salvation?

I remember the first time I was asked that question. I was just beginning my ministry as a pastor. There was a church in our town that somehow knew we were new to the neighborhood and had a couple of members come to visit. Answering a knock on my door, I faced a man dressed in shirt and tie. The man seemed genuinely concerned as he asked me, "If Jesus came today would you have the assurance of salvation?" I smiled. I knew the correct answer (which I gave, of course). Yet after the man left, it hit me: I actually *wasn't* sure! I was a pastor, but I was *not truly sure* of my salvation. I soon learned that I was not alone in this feeling. Many have come to me expressing the same concern.

What about you? Are you *sure* of your salvation? If not, what keeps you from having assurance?

I learned that the top reason given for being unsure—the one I had also given—was "not living up to what I knew I should be living." Of course, I was well acquainted with the problems in my life, especially the ones I was having no success in overcoming. It had become very depressing. It is miserable trying hard to do the right thing only to fail every time, over and over, with no end in sight. Yet, I believed that as long as I could get control over my problems—I mean, let God take my problems—I could be sure I'd be saved. But I never got there. I could only see fault after fault and I was never sure of my salvation.

I found that my problem was not with the specific amount of "dandelions" in my yard; rather, it was my approach to getting rid of them. Like the Pharisees, I viewed my problems as weeds I could clean up. Yet every method I tried only failed. But, in order for any of us to have the right understanding of the way to salvation, we must also have the correct understanding of what keeps salvation away: sin.

I was surprised to learn that my understanding of sin was not in sync with what the Bible taught.* What do *you* think of when you think of sin? What is sin? We usually go to 1 John 3:4 for the definition: "Sin is the transgression of the Law" (KJV). The NIV translates it like this, "Sin is lawlessness." Most would agree that this passage defines sin as disobedience to God's law. And when we normally think of disobedience to a law, we think of behavior, don't we? Then, according to common logic, breaking the law would be "bad behavior," right? So it is natural for us to conclude that if we cut out "bad behavior" from our life—weed-whacking our dandelions—we cut out sin.

Yet, the Bible teaches a very different concept of sin. It starts with a different idea of the law (something that the Pharisees missed). Have you read about how Jesus talked about the law? When questioned about which law was the greatest, Jesus doesn't quote one of the Ten Commandments but instead summarizes the foundation of "all the Law and the Prophets" as loving God and loving your neighbor (Matthew 22:37–40). Jesus taught that the foundational principle of the law is love. Paul also promoted this concept of the law when he wrote, "Love is the fulfillment of the

Law" (Romans 13:10). Now, notice what John says about God: "Whoever does not love does not know God, because God is Love" (1 John 4:8). Jesus and Paul said that the law is about love and John says that God *is* love. Do you see the connection? You cannot fulfill, or keep, the law without love and yet, you cannot love without knowing God. In other words, if sin is lawlessness, it could also be seen as lovelessness, or godlessness. Therefore, the Bible's concept of sin is that, at its core, it is a broken relationship with God; it is living life apart from God.

Please don't misunderstand. This isn't saying that our behavior doesn't matter; it just returns behavior to its correct place. Yes, the results of godlessness will be detected in bad behavior, but bad behavior is not sin, it is the *result* of sin. Sin is separation from God. It is rebellion. It is independence. It is the foundation of the Pharisees' motto: "I can do it myself."

You see, whenever we define sin simply as behavioral, we end up with a bigger problem because behavior is only a symptom of a deeper issue. If we treat the symptom rather than the disease, we will never truly get rid of either. Then, like the Pharisees, we end up focusing only on our behavior, trying to clean ourselves up for others to see. And while some Pharisees may partially succeed in *appearing* spotless, most of us—if we are honest with ourselves— realize that even if we appear clean on the outside, we are still full of disease and rebellion on the inside.

This is like popping off the heads of dandelions to hide your thriving weed issue. Without all those noticeable yellow blossoms littering your yard, you think that you have healthy green grass, but the weeds are still lurking underground. You may have "taken care of" the visible part, but you have neglected the root. And where does God look? He looks at the root: the heart. As a matter of fact, the place God really cares about is the one place we're not able to do anything about. The Bible says we can't change our hearts (Jeremiah 13:23). Thus, by working on the symptoms we are actually fighting the wrong battle in the wrong location, and we will never have victory.

You see, righteousness is not about you gaining control over your behavior but, rather, about you giving up control of your life and depending on God to make you right. Of course, in order to depend on God, you must first get to know Him. This is why you will find in Scripture a relational definition of salvation and of sin, instead of a behavioral definition. Jesus says, "Now this is eternal life: that they may know you, the only true God, and Jesus Christ, whom you have sent" (John 17:3). According to Jesus, salvation is *knowing* God. You can never know anyone without spending time with them, and for this reason, the Bible frequently encourages us to spend time getting to know Him and building a relationship with Him. It makes more sense, then, to conclude that if salvation is knowing God, then sin is *not knowing Him.*

This concept is in direct contrast with the Pharisees' approach to salvation and sin. Since they saw salvation as the reward for good behavior, it was easy for them to correlate bad behavior with sin and condemnation. When Jesus arrived speaking about this relationship concept, they resisted. Accepting His teaching would negate all their hard work. They thought they would look like fools, having struggled to achieve "perfection," only to find such struggles of no value eternally.

Unfortunately, many today still strongly embrace their view of behavior-based righteousness. If you do the right things, or avoid the wrong things, you will be righteous. It is a natural step then to go from the belief that a person can obtain eternal life through behavior to assuming that eternal life can then be lost because of bad behavior. Still, there are many who understand that salvation is a gift that cannot be earned—that it is based on a relationship with God—yet also conclude that salvation can be lost due to misbehavior. How can the means of salvation switch so quickly from relationship-based to behavior-based? If we cannot be saved by mere works alone, why would we be lost by mere works alone?

The Bible is clear that works, *in themselves*, are of no spiritual value. A life of great works, even those done "in the name of God," does not guarantee eternal life (see Jesus' eye-opening parable in

Matthew 7:21–23). Likewise, a life full of bad deeds does not guarantee condemnation (consider the thief on the cross in Luke 23:40–43). Rather, both examples point to a relationship as the deciding factor!

When you understand sin as relationship based, other biblical teachings will make more sense. One such teaching located in Romans 6:23 says: "the wages of sin is death." I had considered this to mean that if we mess up, God punishes us. But this does not harmonize with the Bible's description of God, because it teaches that "in Him we live and have our being" (Acts 17:28). Life is in God; our life is dependent on being *in* Him. Therefore, when we understand that sin is a broken relationship, Romans 6:23 takes on new meaning: it is saying that you can't continue living if you separate yourself from God since He is the source of life. Its not punishment—just reality.

Probably the best illustration I have heard that demonstrates this concept is of the light bulb. We know that a light bulb that is connected to electricity results in light. Without electricity, no light comes from the bulb. So, if you unplug it, the light goes out. Is this the lamp's way of punishing the bulb? No, of course not. It is simply disconnected from its source of power. Likewise, the natural consequence (wages) of disconnecting from our source of life (sin) is death.

Another text, 1 John 3:6, teaches: "No one who lives in him keeps on sinning." Some translations use the word "abide." That is a relationship term. Again, notice the harmony: if whoever lives in Him does *not* sin, what would sin be? Not living in Him. Or, to say it in another way, no one who lives in God keeps on living away from God (sin). This is like saying: no one who is inside the room is outside the room. The point is that when the relationship is repaired you are no longer living in rebellion. Once again, we find another biblical call to a relationship with Christ.

You may be wondering if you can tell whether or not you are in a relationship with God. Let me ask you this: can you know if you are in a relationship with any other person? Yes. Can you tell if you are working on getting to know someone better? Of course. Since you can know these things about your earthly relationships, you can know whether or not you are seeking to become better acquainted with Jesus. Think about it. Can you know if you are spending time trying to get to know Jesus? Absolutely! Then, if you are seeking to know Him better day by day, it is safe to say you have a relationship with Him.

Understand, though, that not all relationships look the same. Some are very close, some are shallow; some have lasted a long time while others have existed only a short time. My relationship with one person can be quite different than someone else's relationship with the same person. We can only do the things we know how to do to build a relationship—through listening, talking, spending time, and seeking to know someone better. If you are doing these things with Jesus, you have a relationship with Him.

Now check this out:

And this is the testimony: God has given us eternal life, and this life is in his Son. He who has the Son has life; he who does not have the Son of God does not have life. I write these things to you who believe in the name of the Son of God so that you may know that you have eternal life. (1 John 5:11–13)

Why did he write this? Not just so you *might* have hope—John said it so you may *know* that you have eternal life. He is telling us how we can have assurance: if we *have* Jesus (relational). You need to grasp the simplicity, and gravity, of this statement. If you don't have a relationship with Jesus, *no matter how good you are* you don't have eternal life. It is not behavioral; it is relational. It is simple and clear—so you can be confident.

Then why is it so difficult for us to be sure of our salvation? The reason we are so confused is because we continue to accept the devil's diversion of defining sin as behavioral. We spend most of our time on the behavioral level—plucking dandelions—but never gaining confidence. Yet, the Bible says as long as we remain in a relationship with Christ, we have life. It is like the man who walked into an elevator in a tall building and asked the elevator attendant, "Will this elevator take me to the top?" "As long as you stay inside," the attendant replied.

You will remain in the relationship as long as *you* don't leave. And when you make the decision to remain in this relationship, Philippians 1:6 means more: "He who began a good work in you will carry it on to completion until the day of Christ Jesus." He started the work in you and He will finish it. This is why cleaning up your yard (behavior) is not your doing. Perfecting a Christlike character in you is *His gift to you*. Your responsibility is to remain connected to Him so He can finish!

Jesus talked about being the vine and us being the branches in John 15. He said that if you abide in Him you will bear much fruit. He doesn't command you to bear much fruit, He commands you to abide. It is a relationship word. He doesn't tell you to focus on the fruit, but to focus on becoming rooted in Him. The fruit is His part. Your part: staying connected.

---

* Lee Venden, "Blessed Assurance." (sermon, Alaska Camp meeting, Palmer, AK, July 17, 2009). I am indebted to Pastor Lee Venden and his teaching on this subject. It challenged me to further study and led to a major change in my understanding on sin.

Chapter Fourteen

"But because of his great love for us, God, who is rich in mercy, made us alive with Christ even when we were dead in transgressions—it is by grace you have been saved."

– EPHESIANS 2:4, 5

Heaven on Layaway

At the end of time a man finds himself standing before the Pearly Gates. Of course, Peter is there to meet him. "Here's how it works." Peter says. "You need one million points to enter into Life. Everything you have done has point value. You just need to tell me what you have done and we'll add them up. If you reach one million points, you can enter."

"Ok," the man said. "Well, I was married to the same woman for fifty years and never once cheated on her."

"That's wonderful," said Peter. "That's worth three points!"

"Three points?" said the man, surprised. "Well, how about this: I attended church all my life and supported many ministries with my money and service."

"Terrific!" said Peter. "That's certainly worth a point."

"A point? Well, I also regularly volunteered at a soup kitchen in my city and established a shelter for homeless veterans."

"Fantastic, that's good for a couple points," said Peter.

"A couple points?" the man cried. "At this rate, the only way I'll get into heaven is by the grace of God."

"Ah! Now *that's* worth one million points!"

In the last chapter, we reviewed the simplicity of the gospel message: If we hold onto Christ, we have life. We read that sin is breaking off this saving relationship with God; it is rebellion against His love. We also found that salvation and condemnation is relational, not behavioral. For some, this probably wasn't good news. Some claim that this is too cheap. Most often, the reason we think this way is because there is a deep desire within us to have something to do with our own salvation. We want to work it out ourselves and be self-made.

Again, this was a constant desire of the Pharisees. It was also something that earned them rebuke. Jesus said that they focused on the wrong areas, neglecting what was most important in their salvation. He cautioned them on their desire to be self-sufficient. They prided themselves on their ability to abide by their own rules of salvation (which are, by the way, the easiest to abide by), yet they neglected more important matters (see Matthew 23:23–26). They lived as though salvation needed to be, and could be, earned. They taught that we must do some pious thing as payment for eternal life. Yet the Bible is very clear that this isn't the case: "But because of his great love for us, God, who is rich in mercy, made us alive with Christ even when we were dead in transgressions—it is by grace you have been saved" (Ephesians 2:4, 5).

God made us alive when we were dead in sin; we are saved by *God's* grace. Just as Peter said in Acts 15:11, "We believe it is through the grace of our Lord Jesus that we are saved." Yes, grace is the real reason we can have this hope of eternal life through a relationship with God.

God's grace is an amazing thing. Most today would define the biblical concept of grace as "unmerited favor" or, as some might suggest, getting what we don't deserve. Interestingly, in the Old Testament, the word for grace is frequently translated "favor" and is found in the commonly used phrase, "[_____] found *favor* in the eyes of the Lord." Noah found favor. Abraham found favor. Moses found favor. The list goes on. I find it fascinating that the favor they each found in God's eyes was unmerited. They didn't *do* anything to deserve it. As a matter of fact, each example has a long enough list of bad behavior on their résumé. Yet, each one was in a relationship with God. Study about their lives and you will see that this favor (grace) came as a result of that relationship.

Although grace was present in the Old Testament, it wasn't fully realized by mankind until Jesus came. John 1:17 says, "For the law was given through Moses; grace and truth came through Jesus Christ." The law was well defined through the writings of Moses. But as Jesus ministered to the people, they were shown a more complete demonstration of grace. Think of the woman caught in adultery—grace. Think of Zacchaeus—grace. Think of the thief on the cross—grace. Undeserved favor had never been seen like this!

Until Jesus, they had, like us, looked back at those who had received God's favor as being worthy of it—as if they had earned it. We often think that those stories served as examples of what would happen if we did the right things. That couldn't be further from the truth. Paul tells us that these stories of men overcoming were to reveal to those who come afterwards the "incomparable riches of [God's] grace (Ephesians 2:6, 7). The stories of human accomplishments in the Bible are to reveal the richness of God's grace to those who lived later. It was not the achievements of men that were on display, but it was the greatness of God's grace. Those stories revealed the grace of a God who is able to save the most imperfect, forgetful backsliders among us.

It was necessary for us to see the greatness of His grace too. Romans 3:23 says, "for all have sinned and fall short of the glory of God." But we cannot stop there; verse 24 continues, "and are justified freely by his grace through the redemption that came by Christ Jesus." We are all sinners, yes. We all fall short of God's glory no matter how hard we try to live "right." And we *all* need to be justified the same way—by His grace! Paul describes it this way:

But when the kindness and love of God our Savior appeared, he saved us, not because of righteous things we had done, but because of his mercy. He saved us through the washing of rebirth and renewal by the Holy Spirit, whom he poured out on us generously through Jesus Christ our Savior, so that, having been justified by his grace, we might become heirs having the hope of eternal life. (Titus 3:4–7)

Our salvation was never based on what we have done, but has always been based on God's mercy—His grace. Repetition of good actions will not create righteousness in our lives. "Conquering" our sinful desires does not earn us a mansion in God's kingdom. Salvation is not earned—it is given. If we are to receive eternal life, it can only be through God's unmerited favor towards us.

Sadly, the mind of a Pharisee isn't satisfied that easily. Surely there is something we must *do* in addition to accepting this grace? Nope. Our works do nothing toward our salvation. The Bible is very clear: we are saved *by grace* (Ephesians 2:8, 9). Period. "And if by grace, then it is no longer by works; if it were, grace would no longer be grace" (Romans 11:6). You can't call it *unmerited* favor if you earn it, can you? It cannot be undeserved if you are able to pay it off in a righteousness installment plan, can it?

Yet, this is what many seem to want: an installment plan on salvation—heaven on layaway. They want eternal life, but do not want it through charity. Yes, it may begin as a gift, but many want to pay God back. Is this what God offers? Salvation: 90-years-same-as-cash? Paul says in Galatians 2:21, "I do not set aside the grace of God, for if righteousness could be gained through the law, Christ died for nothing." If we pass up God's grace and try to work our way to heaven—salvation through a payment plan—we are claiming that Christ's death was worthless! Because, if we can earn salvation by ourselves why did Jesus die?

Now some quickly disagree with this idea. They have told me that they have accepted Christ's sacrifice on their behalf, but there's still a lot of work to do to *keep saved*. Really? Did Jesus go through all of that humiliation and pain, and not change a thing? Did He suffer through everything He did so our salvation would be just as difficult (if not *more)*? Can we truly accept Jesus as our savior and still need to justify ourselves before God with our own actions? This is Paul's answer: "You who are trying to be justified by law have been alienated from Christ; you have fallen away from grace" (Galatians 5:4). Whenever we try to justify ourselves with our own "righteousness" we are in reality distancing ourselves from Christ and abandoning the grace that comes through a saving relationship with Him. What a horrible thought!

Please don't misunderstand this. Living under grace does not mean it doesn't matter what we do. We cannot, as Jude 4 says, "change the grace of our God into a license for immorality." This is not how grace works. Let me give you an example. Imagine you are driving down a highway. You get distracted and are unaware that you picked up quite a bit of speed. You only become aware as you glance in the rear-view mirror and see those pretty blue and red lights closing in on you. Busted! You were speeding and you know it. Although you were clocked going more than 20 mph over the speed limit, for some reason, the officer only gives you a warning. He extends to you unmerited favor—grace. Does this offering of grace allow you to travel the rest of your trip at 20 mph over? If a different officer pulls you over a second time, would you be able to say, "Oh, it's okay officer. I'm driving under grace"? Of course not! Grace does not give us permission to continue to live in rebellion.

What should be our reaction to grace then? The story of Moses provides our answer: Moses was a man who found favor in God's eye. God said so Himself—*to Moses!* This is what Moses said in reply: "You [God] have said, 'I know you by name and you have found favor with me.' If you are pleased with me, teach me your ways so I may know you and continue to find favor with you" (Exodus 33:12, 13).

Upon hearing that God's grace was upon him, he desired to know God *more* so he could continue in that grace. It made him want a deeper relationship with God. Did he ever make a mistake after this? Plenty. Did God's grace still cover him? We know it did: he was on the mount of transfiguration with Elijah and Jesus!

So what happened to his imperfections? Did Moses clear them all up in the last minute? Did he get "control" over his life and that's why he was on that mount with Jesus? Was Moses standing with Elijah because he had proved to God that he was finally worthy? Actually, he disobeyed God right before he died, which resulted in him not entering into the land of Canaan. Even at the end he still had faults. Misbehavior was still part of this great patriarch's life. Yet, he was there, on the mount with Elijah, to encourage Jesus.

Paul's personal struggle can also teach us much about grace. He specifically describes one of his trials as a "thorn in the flesh" that was given to him to keep him from becoming conceited. He says he pleaded with God to take it away three times, yet God wouldn't remove his "thorn." Instead, God gives a very interesting reply to Paul's request: "My grace is sufficient for you, for my power is made perfect in weakness" (2 Corinthians 12:9).

It is clear that Paul was struggling with something. Some have suggested that it was poor vision (mainly because of a statement in Galatians 6:11). However, I have a difficult time believing this was his "thorn." Here's why: most often, when Paul speaks of the "flesh" he is speaking of the sinful nature, not the body itself. So it is more likely that he is talking about a sinful nature issue, not a physical issue. In addition, according to Paul, this issue in his life was there to keep him from becoming conceited. Poor vision, or any other physical impairment, does not necessarily keep someone from becoming spiritually conceited. This had to be something spiritual; possibly some character flaw he wrestled with.

It would make sense that Paul, a former Pharisee, did not like any lagging spiritual problems, so he pleads with God to remove it. Yet, God's reply was, "My grace is sufficient." Would God's grace be needed for poor vision? Is grace simply a bifocal substitute? More to the point, can weak eyesight keep a person out of heaven? Of course not, so why would grace be the solution? Grace is needed for sin. It is required for spiritual "thorns." God's encouragement to Paul was that His grace is sufficient to save a frustrated former Pharisee who was still struggling with spiritual imperfections.

God's grace is sufficient to save sinners, no matter how deep they are in sin. In fact, the greater the sin, the greater the offering of grace (Romans 5:20). Do not underestimate the power of God's grace. His grace was sufficient enough to cover the sins of Adam and Eve, Noah, Abraham, Moses, Rahab, David, Mary Magdalene, Peter, and Paul. His grace was enough for the thief next to Him on the cross—the same one who had no opportunity to clean up his life. And yes, friend, His grace is sufficient to cover you!

You may be thinking, "But you don't know my struggles. You don't understand the issues that plague me." You're right I don't. But there is One who does know and He understands:

> We don't have a high priest who is unable to sympathize with our weaknesses, but we have one who has been tempted in every way, just as we are—yet without sin. Let us then approach the throne of grace with confidence, so that we may receive mercy and find grace to help us in our time of need. (Hebrews 4:15, 16)

Jesus knows what we have been through and knows our struggles. And He is the one offering us grace.

You see, no matter how good you think you are, you will never be good enough. No matter how clean you are, you will never be clean enough. But God already knows that. We always fall short of His glory. Actually, He has never expected us to try to rise to His glory—rising to God's glory is Satan's goal (Isaiah 14:12–14; see also Genesis 3:5)! Instead, God wants you to admit your imperfect humanity—your un-godlike nature—for it is in your weakness, that His strength is revealed.

What if you still have some bumps and bruises? What if you don't have it all together? Lay those imperfections at the feet of Jesus. Trust Him. His grace is sufficient to save you!

Chapter Fifteen

"For we are God's workmanship, created in Christ Jesus to do
good works, which God prepared in advance for us to do."
– EPHESIANS 2:10

God's Handiwork

My father was a carpenter and had all the usual wood-working tools that a craftsman would need down in our basement. Because of his skill and his love for creating things out of wood, I often found myself with wooden versions of toys I had seen and wanted. He made me boats, cars, planes—you name it, he could make it.

One time I saw a sword at a store and really wanted it. It was not just any sword; it was the sword of the (then) popular cartoon character, *He-Man*. My father saw this time as an opportunity to teach me some woodworking skills, so he told to me that although I couldn't buy the one at the store, I could build myself one at home. It was his plan that I would do it—well, most of it—by myself.

He gave me a piece of wood so I could trace the outline of my sword. I took great care in making sure the handle would be just the right size, not just for then, but even as I grew. My dad watched on as I drew out the design, finishing with the blade. All was good, with one exception: I wasn't allowed to make it pointed at the end (something about safety). Instead, he instructed me to round off the tip. The alteration was made and it was ready to be cut out. Due again to safety, I'm sure, my dad guided my hands as I cut the major portions of the design out on the band-saw, while he finished the smaller detail cuts himself.

After a little touch-up with sandpaper, my sword was finally completed! I was so excited about the finished product that I ran around the house pronouncing my newfound power. I learned the satisfaction of creating and building something with my own hands. All was good.

Until one day. . .

I'm not sure anymore what I had done—I've done too many things to really be sure—but I found myself in trouble and facing discipline. This time my discipline would be a spanking. As usual I had to go to my room to prepare (I never figured out what I was actually supposed to do to prepare). My dad came to my room and he had in his hand an item I had not expected. To my horror, he had noticed particular "qualities" of my homemade sword that I had not noticed—it was the perfect shape for a paddle! You can imagine my great distress when, at that moment, the very thing that I had purposely designed and created solely for *my enjoyment* brought me pain instead.

Have you ever made something only to find it being used for something other than what you had planned? If you have, then you know there are few things worse than having something you create used against you. Because everything worth making has been made with a specific purpose in mind.

Did you know that *you* were created for a special purpose? "For we are God's workmanship, created in Christ Jesus to do good works, which God prepared in advance for us to do" (Ephesians 2:10). You are God's workmanship! Isn't that wonderful? And you were created in Christ to do good works.

"Aha!" A Pharisee can be heard saying. "I knew works fit in our salvation somewhere!"

Yes, it is time that we look at our works and see how they fit into this saving relationship with God.

As we have learned, the Bible says very clearly that we are saved *completely* by grace through faith, not by works. Works do not save us, yet we were created to do good works. This seems contradictory, but it isn't.

So what are these "good works," and how can we find out which works *we* were created to do? Some will answer, "Read the Bible." Yes, the Bible reveals a lot of good works, but which of the many good works are *you* supposed to do? All of them? Are you to build an ark too? Or sacrifice your first-born son? Of course not!

Paul says that God "prepares in advance" the works He wants us to do. Therefore, it cannot be just any good works God wants, but good works He designed *just for us*. Much like a screwdriver was designed for screws, you were created for certain good works. Only the One Who created us would know which specific works we were intended to do. In fact, if we examined it closer, we would notice that those previous Patriarchal "works" came from following God's specific requests. And according to Hebrews 11, each of these great works was done in faith.

Faith is another fascinating concept. Without it, "it is impossible to please God" (Hebrews 11:6). And Habakkuk 2:4 says, "The righteous will live by faith." There is no question that it is essential to our spiritual life. However, many today define faith as a religious group or a set of beliefs, or as belonging to a specific church or religion. However, Hebrews 11:1 defines faith as, "being sure of what we hope for and certain of what we do not see."

Faith is also a relationship term. It is based on an experience of past trustworthiness that creates confidence in someone in order to depend on him or her for something you hope for or cannot see. Faith, at its core, is dependence, and it is out of this dependence that our works are to be born.

The Bible reveals that faith and works go together. As James puts it, "Faith without works is dead" (James 4:17). He used the example of Abraham offering up Isaac and said that "his faith and his actions were working together, and his faith was made complete by what he did" (James 4:22). Abraham had confidence in God's promises. His dependence on God had grown so much that if God said something needed to be done, he did it—even sacrificing his promised son.

Think also of Noah. God told him of the coming flood and then revealed the salvational plan of the ark, instructing him to build it and then get inside it. Since Noah had already learned to trust God, he could depend on Him during this time of crisis.

How do we have proof that he depended on God? He built the ark and went inside! We also have proof that the rest of the earth did *not* depend on God. In other words, our actions will reveal in whom we place our confidence and in whom we depend.

Notice, also, this relationship concept in Jesus' teachings: "All who have faith in me will do the works I have been doing and they will do even greater things than these, because I am going to the Father" (John 14:12). Thus, it will be those who have built their confidence in, and placed their dependence on, Jesus that will *do* the works He had been doing.

Jesus further explains this with the illustration of a vine and its branches; He said that He is the vine and we are branches (John 15:1–5, 8). As it goes with grapevines, branches can be grafted into a different vine and grow roots into the new vine and become a part of the vine. The evidence of a successful grafting will be seen when the branch begins to bear fruit. The branch becomes completely dependent on the vine for nutrients and health. In His illustration, Jesus points out that like the vine branch, we too must become fully dependent on Him for spiritual health. The evidence of a successful grafting of our lives into Christ—a *fully* dependent relationship—will be seen in our "fruit." For this to occur, Jesus says that we must remain, or abide, in Him. In fact, separated from Him we can do nothing. This is a powerful image of the type of relationship Jesus desires. Just as bearing fruit is the natural result of being connected to the vine, ultimately, every good work that comes from us is the result of being constantly connected to Christ.

Does this mean that good works do not exist outside of this relationship? No. But just because the works done are considered "good" doesn't mean they are what God requested. Jesus tells this compelling parable explaining:

> Not everyone who says to me, "Lord, Lord," will enter the kingdom of heaven, but only he who does the will of my Father who is in heaven. Many will say to me on that day, "Lord, Lord, did we not prophesy in your name, and in your name drive out demons and perform many miracles?" Then I will tell them plainly, "I never knew you. Away from me, you evil-doers!" (Matthew 7:21–23)

Jesus said He didn't *know* them; He had no *experience* with them. They weren't in this dependent relationship and, as a result, were called evildoers. Christ called their works, which we would normally consider good, evil! Why? According to Jesus, they were not "the will of the Father." This is entirely about depending on God—listening to *Him* and following *His* commands. Works done outside this relationship of faith have no salvational value.

Let me illustrate. Say you are visiting the Grand Canyon and decide at the last minute to hike down into it (not a good last minute plan, by the way). After several hours and a few detours, you find yourself in an unfamiliar area off the beaten path. In spite of all of your efforts to retrace your steps to find the path, you have no luck and unwittingly make yourself more lost. The sun starts to set and the canyon's eerie shadows lengthen around you. As the light fades, it becomes increasingly difficult to recognize anything. Finally darkness sets in, and so does the acceptance that you are completely lost. Unfortunately, all of your efforts, all of your actions, have only made things worse—you're still lost.

More time passes. In your distress, you call out into the cold night air but the only response is a mocking echo of your request. Your voice becomes hoarse. You are about to give up all hope of anyone finding you when, all of a sudden, light fills the canyon wall beside you. A park ranger appears. Your heart leaps for joy! Having seen you wandering off the path hours earlier, the ranger grabbed the necessary items for a rescue and came in after you. The ranger assures you that everything will be alright—he will lead you out to the top of the canyon. All you have to do is follow everything he asks you to do. (And trust him, of course.)

I have two questions: first, when are you rescued—when you reach the top or when you decide to follow the ranger? I'm sure we could agree that the moment of your rescue would be when you decide to follow the ranger. The second question is this: by following the ranger, are you rescuing yourself? No, of course not. You follow the ranger because you are depending on him to take you the rest of the way out. The ranger is in charge of the rescue. Your only "job" is to follow him. Your "works" are listening to and obeying your rescuer.

In other words, I cannot keep the Sabbath to *be* saved, nor do I keep it to *keep* saved. The reality is that God, in Whom I depend, has told me that the Sabbath was made for my benefit, so I *want* to remember it. Likewise, I will stay away from certain things, not because I am trying to rescue myself or am making an effort to look holier to others, but because the One who is actively saving me says I should stay away from those things. If I am dependent on Him I will *do as He says.*

The point is this: your faith is demonstrated in your works. The only way you can show that you are truly dependent on God is by following *Him.* He created you, He's saving you, and He knows what is best for you. You need Him.

Friend, you are God's handiwork! He has created you to do great things in Christ. You have been a part of His plan from the very beginning. Things may have happened. You may have lost your purpose. But He saw you wandering off the path and has come in to seek and to save you. He has come all the way to the bottom of the Grand Canyon of Sin to rescue you and confidently says, "Follow me." However, to be freed from your sins, you will have to completely depend on Him. Then, when you are totally dependent on God, you will do whatever He tells you. You will follow Him. You will trust and obey.

Maybe you still depend on yourself a lot. Maybe you depend too much on a church or a set of traditions. Your actions will reveal the object of your dependence. They may not be evident to the people around you, of course, but God will know. He's the One who designed you and created you for a special purpose. He's the only One who can rescue you out of this dark canyon of sin and restore your life to the purpose for which He created you.

Nevertheless, you are the only one who can make the choice. Will *you* trust Him? Will you abandon the ineffective attempts at saving yourself and, instead, fully depend on Him and follow only Him?

Chapter Sixteen

"Salvation is found in no one else, for there is no other name under heaven given to men by which we must be saved."

– ACTS 4:12

The Great Escape

Far from the crowds, behind closed doors, the meeting began. The air was filled with tension even as the high priest called them to order. The news around town had caused quite a bit of commotion. Therefore, the Pharisees and Chief Priests needed to call a meeting of the Sanhedrin with an agenda to discuss the most recent events. They had received new intelligence that Jesus had performed yet another miracle. This last one was over the top—He raised that guy Lazarus from the dead! It was the last straw! He was becoming too influential. Too many now believed in Him. Their voices betrayed their feelings of frustration as the topic came to its peak: "'What are we accomplishing?' they asked. 'Here is this man performing many miraculous signs. If we let him go on like this, everyone will believe in him, and then the Romans will come and take away both our place and our nation'" (John 11:47, 48).

Jesus was ruining everything. It appeared to them that He could soon destroy everything they had worked for. But, what else could they have done? So far, they were ineffective at removing His influence. What made matters worse was that as His influence increased, theirs decreased. Now they realized that if they were to let Him continue, *Rome* might come and take everything away. Everything *they* had built. Everything *they* worked hard for—*their* place, *their* nation! All on account of this Jesus guy. They had to protect their name. As never before, a dreadful thought ambushed their minds: could their reputation handle this man?

The Pharisees were not the first to be worried about their name and what they had established. In fact, the first time we hear of this concern is not too long after the flood. It is from a story found in Genesis 11.

According to Genesis, the people living just after the flood all spoke one language. Can you imagine how wonderful would that have been—no misunderstandings, nothing lost in translation? During their migration away from the place the ark landed, many settled on a plain in Shinar. While here, they developed a plan to establish a city and build a tower that reaches to the heavens. Now, there is nothing wrong with establishing a city, is there? Of course not; this has happened many times. Nor is it bad to build a really tall tower. But they did not build all of this just for the sake of building. The Bible says that this group wanted to build this city and huge tower to "make a name, lest we are scattered over the earth" (verse 4). Interestingly, before the flood we do not read of this fear of scattering. Of course, before the flood, they hadn't seen God's wrath. Now they *knew* the power of God to punish. They saw the results of God's judgment. So, whom were they afraid would scatter them? God. Then whom else would they be trying to make a name in front of?

Think again about the situation surrounding the flood. It must have been well-known by these people living after the flood that Noah was the only one found blameless in God's eyes before the flood. They knew that his name had gone before God and that he was considered righteous (not through anything Noah did—it was the result of his relationship with God—something these people seemingly forgot). Also, it was through Noah that God brought salvation from the devastation. It would appear, then, that since this group was attempting to make a name before God, they were actually trying to keep from being a part of His wrath again. Only, they were doing it *their* way—trying to save themselves. *They* would make their own name.

And God did notice. He saw the city and tower they were building. It wasn't that the tower was too tall and unsafe. It wasn't that the zoning was wrong for that type of building. Nor was the city getting too big. No, He noticed something far worse. He saw that they were united as a group and had the same language and understanding. This left nothing to hinder what they might plan to do. He says, "If as one people speaking the same language they have begun to do this, then nothing they plan to do will be impossible for them" (verse 6).

We might suppose this meant that God was afraid they might succeed at anything they did, but He doesn't say that. We read that word "impossible" and automatically think that God didn't like what they would be capable of. But the Creator would never fear the created. Actually, this word in the Hebrew gives more of an idea of a fence or a cutoff. In other words, since they were unified and had one language, there was no barrier to what they would try.

Remember, this was about establishing a name before God. It was about attempting to avoid His wrath and save themselves. So there would be no boundary for what they would do to try to save themselves. If God had let them continue in this way, they would have gone so far from the way of redemption that He would not be able to save them. In order to keep salvation possible (mankind seeking Him and calling on His name), God decided to confuse their language (no longer understanding) and scatter them (no longer united). Yes, this is an odd story, but it's an important one, because this was the beginning of a mindset that would continue through the last days.

Babel returns to our attention through the nation of Babylon when Israel was taken captive. Babylon rose to importance not because it was especially noteworthy, but because God used them in His punishment of the Israelites, which was a result of Israel's "unfaithfulness" (1 Chronicles 9:1). 1 Chronicles 5:25 reveals that Israel was unfaithful because they "prostituted themselves to the gods of the peoples of the land." They had forgotten the Lord their God and were unfaithful to Him, so He allowed them to become captives of another nation.

While in captivity, though, the Israelites were also affected by Babylon's ideas. The Babel mindset remained strong in Babylon and can be confirmed in the thinking of King Nebuchadnezzar (before his conversion): "as the king was walking on the roof of the royal palace of Babylon, he said, 'is this not the great Babylon I have build as the royal residence, by my mighty power and for the glory of my majesty?'" (Daniel 4:29, 30)

He believed *he* had established a kingdom and a name. But God rebuked the king for these thoughts. Of course, the nation was no different; they seem to believe that they had succeeded where Babel had failed (see Isaiah 47:7, 8, 10). Furthermore, in spite of being used by God to teach Israel, Babylon abused their power and showed Israel no mercy (Isaiah 47:5, 6). As a result, their actions were judged and their destruction was foretold. In Jeremiah 51:24, God says, "Before your eyes I will repay Babylon and all who live in Babylonia for all the wrong they have done in Zion." Later in the chapter, God says even more about their destruction

Nothing must have struck harder, though, than what God says in Isaiah 14:22: "'I will rise up against them,' declares the Lord Almighty. 'I *will cut off from Babylon her name* and survivors, her offspring and descendants,' declares the Lord" (emphasis mine). The great Babylon was going down. The city had fallen in the sight of God (Isaiah 21:9). And *its name* would be cut off! This was a severe punishment for any who wished to establish a name.

However, God never wanted His people to be a part of the sins of Babylon and its judgment, so He sent them a message: "Leave

Babylon, flee from the Babylonians!" (Isaiah 48:20). Jeremiah 51:6 says, "Flee from Babylon! Run for your lives! Do not be destroyed because of her sins. It is time for the Lord's vengeance; he will pay her what she deserves." This warning was sent out to all of God's people still in captivity to escape the influence and, ultimately, the punishment of Babylon.

Now, you may be wondering what all of this has to do with Pharisees. Nice history lesson, but Babylon was no longer in power in their days. That's true, but the Babylonian mindset had survived. Remember what Jesus rebuked the Pharisees for? A quick review of what we read earlier in Matthew 23 would remind us: everything they did was for themselves—to build up *their* name. Think about it: every law they had written and upheld was created so they could attempt to *escape the wrath of God*. They tried to save themselves and the people. They built a tower of rules that reached the sky! But they went too far:

> You snakes! You brood of vipers! How will you escape being condemned to hell? Therefore I am sending you prophets and wise men and teachers. Some of them you will kill and crucify; others you will flog in your synagogues and pursue from town to town. And so upon you will come all the righteous blood that has been shed on earth, from the blood of righteous Abel to the blood of Zechariah son of Berekiah, whom you murdered between the temple and the altar. (Matthew 23:33–35)

Wow. They killed that last prophet in the Temple! They proved they were willing to do anything to hold on to their power and influence—even kill for it—and became guilty of the blood of the saints in doing so.

Remember the closed-door meeting we read about in John 11? They were frustrated about the growing influence of Jesus and His threat to their name and position, but didn't know what to do about Him. Notice the high priest's solution:

Then one of them, named Caiaphas, who was high priest that year, spoke up, "You know nothing at all! You do not realize that it is better for you that one man die for the people than that the whole nation perish." He did not say this on his own, but as high priest that year he prophesied that Jesus would died for the Jewish nation, and not only for that nation but also for the scattered children of God, to bring them together and make them one. So from that day on they plotted to take his life. (John 11:49–53)

In this passage we see two amazing things. The first thing is that God's plan of Redemption, through Jesus, was to reverse what happened at Babel: He would die "for the scattered children of God, *to bring them together and make them one.*" The second, and most alarming, thing is that killing Jesus was considered their *best plan* in order to keep things as they were.

What does any of this have to do with us? We have learned throughout these chapters that the Pharisees' mentality is still very much in existence today. And, not surprisingly, the book of Revelation warns that the Babylonian mentality would exist until the very end. In fact, in Revelation 17, John saw a woman dressed in purple and scarlet who was glittering with gold, precious stones and pearls. He also saw this written on her forehead: "MYSTERY BABYLON THE GREAT THE MOTHER OF PROSTITUTES AND OF THE ABOMINATIONS OF THE EARTH" (Revelation 17:5). What he saw was the same group represented in the woman, just different clothes.

How will we recognize this group? Jesus tells us in Luke 11:23, "He who is not with me is against me, and he who does not gather with me, scatters." Following Christ creates unity. Thus, anyone purposely causing division is not with Him. Paul further warns:

I urge you, brothers, to watch out for those who cause divisions and put obstacles in your way that are contrary to the teaching you have learned. Keep away from them.

For such people are not serving our Lord Christ, but their own appetites. By smooth talk and flattery they deceive the minds of naive people. (Romans 16:17, 18)

These people are out for their own personal gain and are divisive. Then, in 2 Thessalonians 2:10–12, Paul says that "God sends them a powerful delusion so that they will believe the lie."

This does not mean that God intentionally deceives some into believing a lie. But it is a warning that when people refuse to love and accept the truth and follow only God, they will easily fall prey to deception. This is why the Bible counsels us to study and pray so we might be prepared for any deception that may come. But God is not the one who tempts us. Remember, the Bible is clear that Satan is the father of lies (John 8:44), so it is our adversary that brings any powerful delusion. Although the verse seems to give God credit for sending the delusion, He just allows it to happen.

Paul also says in Romans 1:25, that some "exchanged the truth of God for a lie, and worshiped and served created things rather than the Creator—who is forever praised. Amen." He even warned that there were some throwing the people of God into confusion and "trying to pervert the gospel of Christ" (Gal 1:6–8).

What gospel do they try to pervert? The gospel, simply put, is the gift of salvation in Jesus (John 3:16). Or as Peter says in Acts 4:12, "Salvation is found in no one else, for there is no other name under heaven given to men by which we must be saved." Notice that it has to do with a name.

Why so much emphasis on names? In Matthew 1:21, Mary was to call her son "Jesus" for "he will save his people from their sins." The name Jesus means "the LORD saves"! *His name* is the gospel! Can it get any clearer than that? To remove any doubt, Jesus says in John 14:6, "I am the way and the truth and the life. No one comes to the Father except through me." This is the gospel the Pharisees try to pervert. The gospel is simple: Jesus saves. *There is no other way.* No one else can save us. No doctrine or church can save us. And we *cannot* save ourselves. Only Jesus saves.

The truth is, we can never build up our name before God. But that's okay because we were never supposed to. You see, not long after stopping the people at Babel from "making a name," God promises to make a great name for Abraham (Genesis 12:2). Then, in Isaiah 56:5, God promises to those who follow and obey Him "a memorial and a name better than sons and daughters; I will give them an everlasting name that will not be cut off." (As opposed to having your name "cut off" like Babylon's was.) Furthermore, He promises us a new name in heaven (Revelation 2:17). You don't have to worry about making a name, because if you follow God, He will make one for you! You see, it has never been about our name, it has always been about God's name! Our name can be changed, but His name is sacred and majestic! His name should be made great. His name should be praised. Because *His name saves!* Don't miss this like the Pharisees did.

As God warned in the past, and has also given us a warning in the present (Revelation 14:8; 18:2), this Babylonian/Pharisaic mindset will fall! Friend, being a part of this group—this way of thinking—cannot save you. Instead, anyone in this group will be a part of its judgment.

Yet, some of God's people are still a part of it. You may be one who is still trying to make a name, still trying to reach the heavens on your own, still trying to save yourself. If this describes you, He has a message for you today:

> After this I saw another angel coming down from heaven . . . With a mighty voice he shouted: "Fallen! Fallen is Babylon the Great!" . . . Then I heard another voice from heaven say: "Come out of her, my people, so that you will not share in her sins, so that you will not receive any of her plagues." (Revelation 18:1, 2, 4)

Did you catch that? Escape! Come out of her *my people.* Do not share in her sins. Do not hold on to her mindset. Unfortunately, many have a false sense of security by the conclusion that if they are not part of a certain group or denomination then they are out of Babylon. But the foundation of Babylon is self-preservation. So, if you are holding onto anything for salvation other than Christ (whether a doctrine, a church, a person, or yourself), *you are still held captive in Babylon.* If this describes you, then you need to get out! Escape. Run as far away as possible. Stop thinking that you can save yourself. In other words, quit trying!

Here is the conclusion of the matter—the summary of this book: *Being a better Pharisee cannot save you.* Their very best wasn't even close to being good enough. You can know the right words, worship on the right day, eat the right food, and keep the right doctrines and it is still not enough. No matter how hard you try, you cannot save yourself. So, you must flee from that—quit trying to make a name, quit trying to save yourself, quit trying to be a Pharisee—and run straight to Jesus, *your* Savior! As Paul says in Philippians 3:8, "I consider everything a loss compared to the surpassing greatness of knowing Christ Jesus my Lord, for whose sake I have lost all things. I consider them rubbish, that I may gain Christ and be found in him."

This is the great escape: *completely* surrendering to your Lord and Savior, Jesus Christ. Friend, today is the day of salvation. Today you must make your choice. Today is the day to start, or renew, your dependent relationship with Jesus. It is time to leave Babylon and the Pharisee way of thinking. It is time to escape—right into the arms of Jesus!

"Now there was a man of the Pharisees named Nicodemus,
a member of the Jewish ruling council.
He came to Jesus at night. . ."

– JOHN 3:1, 2

Memoirs of a Former Pharisee

He was exhilarated, anxious and embarrassed all at the same time. Glancing around, attempting to avoid any spying eyes, he headed for the rendezvous point. He was torn inside. On the one hand, he hoped nobody would find out about this secret meeting. On the other hand, he was ashamed that he was not brave enough to have this meeting in public—during the day, even!

Yet, at that moment, the thrill of meeting *Him* took over. He couldn't even remember the last time he was this excited. He had heard so much about this mysterious rabbi and now, much to his surprise, Jesus agreed to meet with him. If some of the other Pharisees and Jewish leaders learned of this, his career was as good as over. So there he was, under the cover of night, about to meet face to face with the One who would change his life.

As hard as Nicodemus might have tried to keep it a secret, it is evident that the news of this meeting got out (since it *is* recorded in John 3). This wasn't because Jesus would have tattled on him, nor was it because there were biblical Paparazzi hiding in the bushes to get the juiciest stories for the soon to be written "New" Testament. Rather, it was because there would be no reason to keep it a secret later in Nicodemus' life.

This nighttime meeting occurred near the beginning of Jesus' ministry. At the end of John 2, we are told that as a result of what Jesus taught and the miracles He did during the Passover feast many began to believe in Him. Sometime soon after this feast we are introduced to this Jewish leader, Nicodemus. He seems to be the spokesperson for a group of the Pharisees who, at the very least, were curious about learning more about Jesus. Nicodemus' opening comment revealed a lot: "Rabbi, we know that you are a teacher who has come from God. For no one could perform the signs you are doing if God were not with him" (John 3:2). Notice he said "we." He doesn't provide a list of names, but there were definitely others.

Although we do not know how many were included in the "we," there was a group among the leaders who believed in Jesus from the early days of His ministry. Yet, they were a secret group. They were afraid to openly admit their belief. In John 12:45, we are told that even those in this leadership group were scared of being kicked out of they synagogue by the other Pharisees if they were open about believing in Jesus.

But on that particular evening Nicodemus took the first step: he met with Jesus. Others may have wanted to, but he did it. He may have shared what he heard from Jesus with the others later, but right then, he talked directly to Him. It was the best decision he could have ever made. For that night was the beginning of the change in his life. That evening, Jesus explained to him the full gospel. Consider some of the things Jesus told him:

> Very truly I tell you, no one can see the kingdom of God
> unless they are born again. . . . unless they are born of

water and the Spirit. . . . Just as Moses lifted up the snake in the wilderness, so the Son of Man must be lifted up, that everyone who believes may have eternal life in him. For God so loved the world that he gave his one and only Son, that whoever believes in him shall not perish but have eternal life. For God did not send his Son into the world to condemn the world, but to save the world through him. (John 3:3, 4, 14–17)

One of the most memorized verses in the Bible (John 3:16), which contains the full gospel in its simplicity, was shared with Nicodemus that night. Can you imagine the impact it must have had to hear that for the first time? Long before "3:16" would be painted on sport enthusiasts' chests in packed stadiums, Nicodemus would bring back to his fellow believers a powerful message: Jesus is the One who would save them. Talk about a life-changing message! Jesus didn't waste words.

This was where the change in Nicodemus' life began—in that personal meeting with Christ. Sure, it might have been a secret meeting at night, but *he met with Christ!* Everything was different for Nicodemus after that night. I can imagine him returning to the other under-cover believers and their questions: "What did He say? Tell us everything!" I wonder if they regularly met together secretly or determined to keep their distance as to not draw any attention. Either way, it appears that Nicodemus continued thinking about what Jesus taught him. Maybe he even caught more of Christ's teachings from the crowd. It was not long, however, until we read of him again—at another secret meeting.

This time, it's not night and he's not meeting with Jesus. It was behind closed doors in a meeting of the Pharisees. John 7:32 tells us that some of the Pharisees caught wind that more people were beginning to believe that Jesus was the Messiah, so the group had sent temple guards to arrest Him. However, as we learned earlier, the guards didn't arrest Jesus because "no one ever spoke the way this man does" (John 7:46). A discussion ensued. The Pharisees were visibly agitated. It was suddenly clear to them that there must be a curse on everyone else, since they, themselves, knew better than to believe in Jesus.

Then Nicodemus spoke up. Previously, he snuck out into the night to secretly meet with Jesus, but this time he spoke up to a group of irritated Pharisees (I'd say that was a change!). He asked the group an honest question: "Shouldn't we meet Him and hear what He has to say before we make a judgment about Him?" (John 7:51). Even though it was a simple question, there was something more to it. It is possible that he was just trying to be fair, but it is also quite likely that he knew what could happen if they actually listened to Jesus and heard him for themselves. If it happened to him, it could happen to them. This may have been a covert witnessing opportunity—casting a stealthy net. Either way, this time Nicodemus spoke up! He was coming to Jesus' defense. It may not seem like much, but this would have taken a lot of courage—especially in that situation, in a tense room filled with Jesus haters!

They responded by mocking Nicodemus and attempting to set him straight. What may have appeared to be a victory for them had actually prompted Nicodemus to the next step in His walk with Christ: speaking up for Him. He didn't fly off to a mission field or hold evangelistic meetings in a packed stadium—he may not have even stood up for Jesus adequately in the meeting—but he stood up. Even in his fear, he humbly suggested that they get to know Jesus for themselves. He was changing—a little less Pharisee, a little more disciple of Christ.

After this conflict, we don't read about Nicodemus for awhile. The next time he appears in the story was during another dark moment. It was again at night. However, this time, it was not for a secret meeting. Jesus was dead.

In John 19:38, Joseph of Arimathea asked Pilate for Jesus' body. It mentions that Joseph was another secret disciple as well, due to a disabling fear of the Jewish leaders. When he received permission, another man joined him to help take his body away: Nicodemus.

Nicodemus brought with him a mixture of myrrh and aloes. When they got to the tomb, Nicodemus helped Joseph wrap Jesus' body in linen, along with the spices, as the custom was.

Some have suggested that Nicodemus was just acting in basic Pharisaic piety. However, the Pharisees clearly hated Christ and would never have sanctioned something like this. His gesture would have been a personal choice. A choice, though, that could not be hidden. Just the amount of myrrh and aloe alone would have drawn attention: it was about 25 pounds worth. This was a typical amount to prepare a king for burial. It is evident that by this time in his life, Nicodemus saw Jesus as the true King of the Jews.

Furthermore, he helped carry Jesus' body from the cross, helped wrap Him and then helped lay Him in the tomb. The man who first came to Jesus at night afraid was now openly caring for the body of his Master. A "pretend" follower would never go to this length. With despair and defeat in his heart, he helped lay the One who was supposed to save him in a tomb. The Savior who died unjustly; the Messiah who had promised to set him free, cut down. The Promised One from God, now in a tomb. How could this be? At that moment, all seemed lost.

I wonder if, after the morning of the third day when Jesus rose victorious, Nicodemus was one of the many people to whom Jesus appeared (Acts 1:3). Regardless, we do not read of Nicodemus again (at least not specifically). There are no books written about his many missionary trips, or letters written by him to recently established churches needing encouragement and correction. Yet there is evidence that he continued following. He must have sat down with the Apostle John and told his story. How else would we know of all of those secret meetings? John wasn't there with him and Jesus that night; he wasn't in the secret Pharisee meeting; he wasn't there helping to bury Jesus with Joseph. John was able to document these stories because he was told these stories—stories from a changed man—a former Pharisee.

Nicodemus may not have been the first Pharisee to step out and follow. He surely wasn't the last. He was one among many.

Acts 15:5 reveals that several from among the Pharisees became followers of Christ. He wasn't even the most popular. Paul, the prolific writer of letters in the New Testament, major missionary, and church planter, was also a former Pharisee (Acts 23:6).

Still, Nicodemus' story can fill us with hope. He was timid and afraid, yet that's where Jesus met him. He was slow to start, yet kept following—even if from a distance. This once-legalistic man started as a closet believer and became a documented convert. His is a story of the effect Jesus can have on us if we will just follow Him. Even the most timid following, or a newly budding interest for a relationship, can change a life! A life that now follows Christ, listens to Him, and stands up for Him—even if secret, hesitant, and gradual at first. It is a life that becomes less a Pharisee and more a disciple. Hopefully his story has encouraged you, above all else, to take that first step to meet with Jesus (a great place to start is by reading or re-reading the Gospel of John) and listen to Jesus with an open heart and mind.

It's a simple start, but that meeting will change your life.

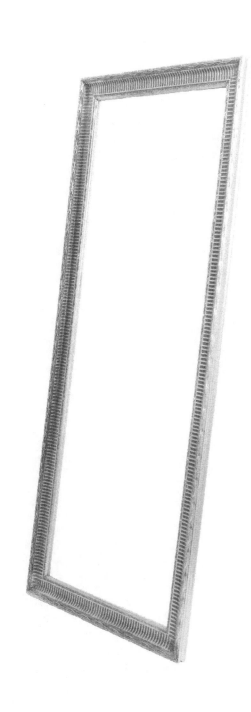